WEAPON OF A.S.S. DESTRUCTION

BY ALFONZO "ZO" RACHEL

WHITE HALL PRESS
Powder Springs, GA

Weapon of A.S.S. Destruction

by Alfonzo Rachel

Published by:

> White Hall Press
> 3150-A Florence Road, Suite 2
> Powder Springs, GA 30127–5385
> www.whitehallpress.com

Except the Ten Commandments, quoted from the KING JAMES VERSION, all Scripture quoted from the NEW AMERICAN STANDARD BIBLE®, Copyright © 1960, 1962, 1963, 1968, 1971, 1972, 1973, 1975, 1977, 1995 by The Lockman Foundation. Used by permission.

Printed in the United States of America.

Text design by Justus Stout and Michael Minkoff, Jr.
Cover design by Joseph Darnell and Michael Minkoff, Jr.

ISBN: 978-1-4675-0255-9

PRAISE

Alfonzo is my new favorite Republican.

 –ANN COULTER, social/political commentator

Alfonzo represents the rugged individualism this country was founded on. Every time I watch one of his videos I want to stand up and salute. I see in him the same stuff the founding fathers are made of. He's one of the most multi-talented, multifaceted, and one of the bravest bastards I know.

 –ANDREW BREITBART, late political maverick

Zo's distillations are breathtaking and so funny... I was stunned for hours by the most provocative, riveting and cohesive social statements I've read in the last twenty years. Zo touched, in some way... everything... with such focus and force... I laughed so hard on the plane people thought I was crazy!

 –DWIGHT SCHULTZ, Actor: *A-Team, Star Trek*

Zo has powerful things to say, and he says them in such a straightforward, honest, and truthful way that the sound you hear ringing in your ears is simply the ring of truth, clearly and bravely uttered.

 –BILL WHITTLE, social/political commentator

Zo's message is always creative, inspirational, informative, and entertaining. Whether he's singing it, preaching it, or just telling it like it is, he's not only "right" but right on time. We're blessed to have him on our side.

 –AL SONJA SCHMIDT, former writer for *In Living Color*

What's always fascinated me about Zo is the fact that he's funny without ever making jokes. Most of the time he's just disassembling the opposition with a sort of good-natured logic. I don't even know why it's amusing, but it is. Maybe because the left's reasoning is so silly that, when Zo exposes it, its natural absurdity comes out. In any case, the guy is just a pleasure to spend time with.

 –ANDREW KLAVAN, best-selling author

Special thanks to my God, and thanks to my woman!

–Zo

CONTENTS

CHAPTER 1

THE SO-CALLED PARTY SWITCH

Although we constantly hear the phrase, "The winners are the ones who write history," this is not necessarily the case. Sometimes it's sore losers with strong grudges who position themselves to brainwash people with their *victim-speak*. They're often bullies who were oppressing others, and when they get pried off of their victims, they act like they're the ones who are being wronged.

Unfortunately, too many people buy it, allowing themselves to be manipulated by those who think they should have control over other people's lives in some fashion. It doesn't take long to realize that Liberal historians are like spoiled children who are always trying to change the game when things don't go their way. Since they always find that they're on the wrong side of history, they try to reword it to suit their needs.

Knowing this, it makes sense that liberals flock to careers in journalism and the public education system. Democrats want to be in control of what we think—how we perceive conservatives, and especially how we perceive *Democrats*. Sadly, too many conservatives let 'em get away with it. The problem grows because we ignore them and underestimate the liberal agenda. At first, I thought conservatives didn't like the idea of cutting and running. I thought conservatives wouldn't bury their heads in the sand. Sure, the conservatives may get tough on elected officials, but they won't confront the culture that votes these liberals into office in the first place.

This is a wake-up call to conservatives, and, yes, that includes the Tea Party. While you're facing off the liberals in government, you've got your back turned to the culture that puts them in power. You have to learn to connect with the culture, or at least know how to turn liberal weapons against the liberals who wield them.

LIBERALS: *People who demand conveniences at the expense of others*

Liberals have been using the same accusations for decades, mind you, and conservatives have had decades to form rebuttals to these same, tired talking points. They accuse conservatives and Republicans of the same racism they've been accommodating right in front of people's faces, successfully convincing a considerable amount of people along the way that it's always been the right wing. This can't continue.

2

Liberals have been able to establish their lies through repetition, and conservatives must have the stamina to be as repetitive in the truth as liberals are in their lies. But like I said, we too often turn a blind eye, saying that there are more important issues. Meanwhile, liberals wage their assault that stigmatizes the right wing, effectively type-casting conservatives as prejudiced, creating huge obstacles to the reception of conservative ideas. But if we leave the cultural arena to liberals, we accept the cycle of a culture that hates conservatism, and we'll only get more of this hatred as the people elect representatives who espouse their own hatred of conservatism.

Historically, the Democratic Party has been consistently racist—endorsing slavery and opposing civil rights.

Conservatives have to be relentless to penetrate prejudice and to show the people who the real culprits have been. We need to constantly drill it. Make liberals face the truth before they make you out to be what they want others to believe you are. Fire, reload, and fire again with the most convicting historical truths concerning Democrats. So, let's see if we can clear the fog concerning some things the Left has tried to get people lost in, starting with the supposed big party switch between Republicans and Democrats.

Historically, the Democratic Party has been consistently racist—endorsing slavery and opposing civil rights. But whenever this is brought to the attention of liberals, they vaguely point to a party change in the last 150 years, saying that what once was the Democratic Party is now the Republican Party, and vice versa.

3

Switching sides of the political aisle never happened, at least, not as they describe it. I'll get to that. What did happen, however, is that the *black community* made a big party switch. The black demographic used to vote for the Republican Party, but as you read on, we'll explore their switch to the Democratic Party.

Racist Past of the Democratic Party

Despite what you've probably been told your whole life, it was the Democratic Party that fought to keep slavery legal and that worked to impose the Jim Crow laws and the Dred Scott decision. They were Democrats who founded the KKK as a terrorist fraternity against the abolitionist Republicans and the blacks they stood for. Democrats revoked federal office positions held by blacks. Go ahead and look up the policies of Democrats like Woodrow Wilson. I'll wait...

...You back? See, what'd I tell you? Wilson even had a White House showing of the pro-KKK movie *Birth of a Nation*.

They were Democrats who fought for segregation in the schools and in the military. They were Democrats who bombed the churches that had a noticeable amount of black members. They were Democrats who hosed peaceful civil rights assemblies and released dogs on them. You'll probably recognize Bull KKK Connor out there. Yes, he was a Democrat *and* a member of the Ku Klux Klan.

All the things Martin Luther King Jr. was fighting against were inflicted by the Democratic Party. When King was put in jail, who do you think put him in there? Democrats. Who do you think imposed the legislation that forced people like Rosa Parks to give up her seat for whites and go to the back of the bus? Democrats. Black people had been so successfully disenfranchised by the Democratic Party that John F. Kennedy (a northern senator who opposed civil rights, mind you) had MLK released from jail, and the black community was then so happy with him that they forgot that Democrats jailed MLK in the first place.

They forgot about the Republican President Dwight Eisenhower who sent military support to make sure that black kids could go to school. He also pressed to desegregate the military. He put into action what the Democrat Harry Truman only put on paper. Truman was also a member of the Ku Klux Klan, he just didn't attend their slumber parties. Or so he says.

I hear sad theories about how blacks feel like the Republicans threw them under the bus in some unwritten deal in the 1877

4

Compromise known as the Corrupt Bargain. Now I admit, at first glance, it sounds like a harsh deal—but let me explain.

Rutherford B. Hayes emerged from the Civil War as a brigadier general (he later was brevetted major general), a war hero who had been wounded five times, and a member of Congress. In Congress, from 1865 to 1867, Hayes consistently supported radical Republican reconstruction measures which included the Fourteenth Amendment and the setting up of radical Republican regimes in the South.

This was the situation: Ruthy B. would get the White House if he would agree to withdraw the union troops from their southern occupation, which would leave blacks defenseless. But hold on a second—leave them defenseless against whom? Oh yeah! The Democrats. Democrats were the ones blacks needed the protection from. Even then, it wasn't like Hayes just handed blacks over to the Democrats by withdrawing the Union troops. The hand-shake deal was that the Democrats would honor the rights of blacks.

5

Keep in mind, the so-called Corrupt Bargain was an unwritten deal, meaning there is no formal record of it. However, what *is* on record is that Rutherford B. Hayes was a staunch abolitionist who defended blacks pro bono against the Fugitive Slave Act, signed in by Democratic President Thomas Jefferson.

Ruthy B. also endorsed the impeachment of President Andrew Johnson. Remember, y'all, Andrew Johnson was the Democratic president who revoked Sherman's Field Order No. 15 during the March to the Sea. That's the forty acres and a mule order that Republican President Lincoln approved. So, for the Afrocentrics that are still demanding their forty acres and a mule, you should be angry only at the Democrats.

Y'all might be wondering why a racist like Andrew Johnson would be Lincoln's vice president. That's because, as y'all know, the preservation of the Union was paramount to Lincoln. In fact, it was more important than freeing slaves, because if the Union dissolved, slaves could forget about their freedom altogether. Though pretty much all Democrats were pro-slavery, some of them were not pro-secession. This is where Andrew Johnson comes in: Johnson was pro-slavery, but he was also staunchly in favor of protecting the Union from disintegration. Though Lincoln was anti-slavery, he was able to use Andrew Johnson's policies to his advantage. Because of Johnson, he was able to rack up some southern votes. Yes, perhaps a southern strategy of sorts.

In light of all of this, you can see that Rutherford B. Hayes and the Republican Party in general are on record risking their political careers and their lives for black freedom for years, whereas the Democrats were ostracizing and oppressing black people. So why is it that something that's not even on record (the 1877 Compromise) convinces us that the Republicans deserve the heave-ho? I understand black people felt as if the heave-ho was what *they* got, but even if that were the case, why don't we look at who backed us into a corner in the first place? That would be the Democrats. Democrats have always been ravaging the black community, and Republicans always get the blame for it. Not a single thing has changed in over 150 years.

DIVIDE AND CONQUER

Now, after we've made the hard-hitting case of the history of Democrat bigotry, the liberals and Afrocentrics will try to use some cockamamie excuse that the Democrats and Republicans switched sides, and the Republicans today are what used to be the Dixiecrats. But even before this so-called switch (and we'll get to that), blacks had already started voting for the Democratic Party. So come on, y'all. What was the reason they started voting for the Democrats before the so-called big switch?

Divide and conquer, y'all! Haven't you ever heard of that strategy? The Democrats divided blacks from the Republican Party and corralled them for their voting stock by seducing them with entitlements. Blinded by disenfranchisement, the black community couldn't even see that their loyalty was being bought ever so cheaply by the very ones who were oppressing them. *Look here, Negro: you can't eat here, and you can't go to school there, but here's some food stamps so you can feel good about it. The Republicans would never do that for ya!* The black community has been sold on the idea that entitlements are more valuable than dignity.

Even when the Republicans had a majority vote ready to pass the civil rights act, the Democrats filibustered the bill. Now the liberals will try to give Lyndon B. Johnson the credit for this, post facto. But LBJ can be credited for another agenda: he said he was dead set on having those n-words vote for Democrats for the next 200 years. You liberals want to believe there was a southern strategy so bad? Well, there it is. LBJ clearly laid it out for you. Republicans wanted blacks to have civil rights for one simple reason: it's their civil right. LBJ wanted blacks to have civil rights because he wanted to use them to keep Democrats in power.

> The black community has been sold on the idea that entitlements are more valuable than dignity.

7

This wasn't the first time blacks were used for their votes. LBJ's agenda harkens back to the Constitutional patriarchs of the Democrat Party. Even though pro-slavery founders viewed their slaves as property and not people, they would still count them as people in the census in order to gain more pro-slavery representation. That's pretty sick, ain't it? Count the slaves as people only to get more representation for legislation that would ultimately make them property instead of people. Yeah, Democrats are sick. LBJ was the same way. He wanted blacks to have civil rights only in order to empower the Democratic Party—to keep the black community as their faithful voting stock.

Now, when you tell backward-thinking liberals all this, they start squirming. They're losing the game, and like a spoiled rotten kid they'll try to twist the game. And here it comes y'all! Here comes their twisted response to everything you just told them because they refuse to face the truth about the Democrats:

Say it with me: *Well, the parties have switched, and the Republicans of today used to be the Dixiecrats.*

8

Okay, let's break this down. First of all, they won't really acknowledge the bigoted history of Democrats. If you're going to assert that there was a switch, then you have to admit that the Democrats had been the racist party in the first place—but you won't, because you got nowhere to go from there. You've got no good explanation for why the black community started voting for Democrats long before the so-called big party switch. But that's okay. I've already told ya why that happened a few paragraphs back. In a nutshell, the black community was bamboozled into voting Democrat and are still hoodwinked and co-opted today.

Secondly, their response begs the question: was the big party switch a mutual switch? I mean, did Republicans get up and walk over to the Democrat side, and Democrats get up and walk over to the Republican side? That would be an amazing display of cooperation between the two parties, wouldn't it?

Now, it is true that some Democrats were seen as going soft on racism, but the staunchly racist Democrats became known as Dixiecrats, and that's as far as they went. Those Dixiecrats did not transition over to become Republicans. They returned to the Democratic Party. Dixiecrats declared that they would rather vote for a "yellow dog" than vote for a Republican because the Republican Party was known as the party for blacks. Let me introduce you to the crowd that returned to the Democratic Party after the so-called switch:

> Gov. Benjamin Laney AR,

> Gov. Frank Dixon AL,

> Gov. Hugh White MS,

> Gov. William Murray OK,

> Gov. Sam Jones LA,

> Gov. Fielding Wright MS,

> US Sen. James Eastland,

> US Sen. John Stennis,

> US Rep. John Williams,

> US Rep. William Colmer,

> Walter Sillers MS S.O.H.

There you go—*some*. It should also be pointed out that those in the Republican Party who showed favor to Dixiecrat ideals got thrown out... *ahem* *Trent Lott*. However, those who were in high ranking positions in the KKK are just fine by the Democrats... *ahem* *Robert Byrd*.

It should be very evident now that the modern Republican party is *not* made up of racist Democrats who decided to switch aisles, but even during their death croak, liberals will still try to point to David Duke as proof of the opposite. David Duke was a lifelong Democrat who tried to save his career by running as a Republican as a last resort. He even tried to run as a Populist before running as a Republican. When he finally did get elected it wasn't because he relied on old Dixiecrat ideals—it was his stance against property taxes that resonated with Republicans. You should take note that Ronald Reagan and George H. W. Bush did not back old David Dukie.

Even if there were a few Dixiecrats that did switch to the Republican side of the aisle and stayed, they would have been Democrats who no longer agreed with the bigotry of the Democrat party and became Republicans. I say this because the Republican Party is the one that passed the civil rights act. Therefore, if anything, the Republican Party would be including Democrats that had a change of heart.

10   To sum it up, rabidly racist Democrats became Dixiecrats and walked out on the less-hardened Democrats, but eventually went back to the Democrat party. They did not become Republicans. The ones who became Republican voted on changed principles. Strom Thurman is one of those Democrats that changed his tune on racism and became a Republican. Remember, if he wanted to stay a racist he could have just stayed with the Democrats. Things worked out better for them anyway.

Liberals will try to dig up anything they can to shine their cherry-picked example of Strom Thurman, and present him as the proof that there was this huge adjustment between Democrats and Republicans. Democrats held Strom Thurman in suspicion and maligned his motives for switching; if he would have remained a Democrat, however, the liberals and the Afrocentrics would have given him a pass, made excuses for him, and overlooked his bigoted history, just like they did with Robert Byrd. Byrd would have been completely vilified by the liberals and Afrocentrics had he become a Republican, but he was given a pass for remaining a Democrat.

THE TRUTH IS OUT

Democrats throughout history are on record proving that their agenda is to control the black population in some form, and that they will approve entitlements for the black community to keep them as loyal Democratic voters. Of course, if you ask a liberal, any time Republicans do anything in favor of the black community, there has to be some sort of angle to it. It's never because the Republican Party stands for freedom and equality.

So. There's an examination of the so-called party switch. Liberals look insane to me as they speed around in illogical circles. They are desperately trying to prove that the Republican Party is racist by using dubious, cherry-picked events—all the while ignoring the full racist tree of the Democrat Party. Hey, liberal! Back up from that tree you're hugging. You might see the forest. Next let's take a look at this business about the switch between liberals and conservatives.

11

CHAPTER 2

LIBERALISM ≠ LIBERTY

eing American means something different to everybody. I've heard people say, *Why can't we all forget
political divisions and just be Americans?* Well, what
does it mean to hold to traditional American values? Where is
our standard for holding true to our roots of good government?

Is the standard found in the Declaration of Independence? Or
the Constitution? Let's say it's both. But now we have another
dilemma: by what standard do we interpret these documents? I
promise I'm gettin' somewhere with this.

Do I rely on a constitutional scholar? Well, Obama's supposed
to be a constitutional scholar, but his thoughts on the Constitution are that it needs a fabulous makeover. Since he can't do
away with the Constitution, which is what he would really like,
he just reads it as if were upside-down and backwards.

Since so many people are going to reshape the Constitution in
order to suit themselves, I can't rely on interpretations made by
people. Instead, I must rely on insight from the One who grants
us our unalienable rights in the first place—God.

The true meaning of *conservatism* is the conservation of our
God-given rights. That's what it really means to be conservative,

despite how Democrats have tried to twist its perception over the years.

A conservative interpretation of the Constitution will align with the Declaration of Independence, affirming that "all men are created equal, that they are endowed by their Creator with certain unalienable Rights, that among these are Life, Liberty, and the pursuit of Happiness." Did you notice that it doesn't say *All men are equal*, or even *All men are born equal*. It says "created equal," which means that our right to life, liberty, and the pursuit of happiness is a result of being created. It wasn't by chance that the founders used the word *created*. The men who drafted the documents that founded our nation understood that human liberties are not a product of government policies, but rather, they are evident because of the way God created the world.

14 WHAT HAPPENED TO LIFE AND LIBERTY?

The founding fathers knew that tyrannical governments would, if they were not restrained, abuse their power and disregard people's right to life—like children cut from their mother's bellies as if the fetus never had the right to live. Liberal interpretation of the Constitution not only legalizes abortion, but it even allows the government to force you to pay for someone else's abortion. But that shouldn't surprise us, as the Democratic Party has historically proven to be the party of eugenics, anti-miscegenation, and segregation. The only thing they wanted to conserve was the white race, but they've tried to cover their tracks with their new, utopian feel-goodism theme of diversity.

Democrats are liberals who take gross liberties when interpreting the Constitution, and the result is a ratified selfishness which imposes the benefit of some at the cost of others. A liberal interpretation of the Constitution allows one group of people to make another group of people their property and forcibly enslave them. Of course, I'm referring to the early Democratic stance on slavery.

Now, when I bring up the Constitution and tell people that I'm trying to return to its principles of liberties, I get a lot of people really mad. In fact, one of the reasons Afrocentrics hate Republicans is *because* they stand closest to the Constitution. You see, Afrocentrics have been led to believe that the Constitution is a pro-slavery document, and that it refers to blacks as three-fifths of a human being. Talk about taking liberties with interpretation!

The three-fifths clause was put into the Constitution by the anti-slavery patriarchs of the abolitionist Republican Party in order to make sure that Indians who had no allegiance to America weren't being counted in the census by the proponents of slavery (namely, the patriarchs of the Democratic Party). The proponents of slavery were not only trying to count their slaves in order to get more representation, they were even trying to include the Indians of other tribal nations so that they could have more representation as a slave state. The anti-slavery founders retorted with the three-fifths policy, including Indians in the American census only if that Indian was paying at least three-fifths of the taxes that all other "American" persons paid. That's why it says in the Constitution, "Excluding Indians not taxed, three fifths of all other Persons."

15

The liberal agenda is always trying to portray the Constitution as a pro-slavery document, convincing Americans that the Constitution isn't helpful for achieving liberty; however, this is the same liberal mindset that had previously twisted the meaning of the Constitution so that they could *legalize* slavery.

Liberals will even try to lay some sort of claim on Lincoln by saying he was a liberal. It's hard to prove that when you look at

WEAPON OF A.S.S. DESTRUCTION

the Republican platform he ran on. Lincoln was a conservative. He represents those who wanted to conserve the Constitution from the Democrat's perversion of it by interpreting the Constitution in a way that made it illegal to forcibly deprive some-one's life, liberty, and property for the benefit of another. Take a look at the Republican platform of 1860. That's the platform that Lincoln ran on. This platform was made according to the conservative interpretation of the founding documents. Lincoln was a liberator, not a liberal.

Lincoln was a *liberator*, not a liberal.

Can you detect a common theme in liberal thinking now? Just as a liberal interpretation made the self-serving argument that some people don't qualify as human and made them slaves, even today they disqualify the humanity of children in the womb for selfish convenience.

16

WHAT HAPPENED TO THE PURSUIT OF HAPPINESS?

A liberal approach to politics leads to more income taxes, even though the Constitution doesn't speak of a general income tax. Now, there are duties and excises and such, but not general income taxes. The Constitution says that Congress can collect the taxes listed to "Pay the Debts and provide for the common Defense and general Welfare." But what does "general welfare" mean? Well, the general welfare of the United States originally had a lot to do with how well she was defended. The modern, liberal interpretation, however, assumes that providing for the general welfare means the that government's job is to provide housing, food, healthcare, etc. Not true! The welfare of this country is in making sure that freedom is defended so that we may conduct our own pursuits.

The founding fathers didn't want the government funded by income taxes because they knew the government would bleed the people dry and the country would go broke. (You know, kinda like we are now.) That's why the income tax wasn't initially in the Constitution. It was later introduced in the Sixteenth Amendment under the guise of clarification. But there was nothing to clarify! The founders left it out on purpose.

The income tax isn't the only liberal agenda being pushed by unconstitutional means. The Constitution currently stipulates that taxes levied should be uniform throughout the United States. Uniform! You know, meaning you can't tax one product, or service, or income differently from another.

17

Liberals have a vendetta against cigarettes, even though a lot of them smoke. I'm not crazy about cigarettes either, but I don't agree with higher taxes on them. Such tax discrimination seems to verge on legislating morality, doesn't it? Taxes are supposed to be uniform. Liberals have a similar vendetta against the rich. They push for higher taxes on the rich *because* they are rich; but taxes are supposed to be uniform. You can't constitutionally tax one income bracket differently than another.

See, the Constitution talks about the uniformity of taxes, *not* the uniformity of profit or wages. Liberals have decided to cut-and-paste the Constitution to get what they want. So liberals! Stop trying to cut everybody down to what you have arbitrarily determined is a comfortable income bracket. Shouldn't we be free to earn as much as we're willing to work for?

WEAPON OF A.S.S. DESTRUCTION

The liberal view of America is that, since it's a free country, everything should be exactly that—free. But, since nothing is free, the left wing settles to have their comforts and their conveniences given at the expense of others. The Left has always taken advantage of systems like slavery, entitlements, benefits, and abortion to provide for some at a high expense to others.

"GIVE ME YOUR TIRED, YOUR POOR, YOUR HUDDLED MASSES. WE COULD USE THEIR VOTES."

Have you ever realized how liberals are constantly trying to make America more like countries that other people risk their lives to leave? But it doesn't look like any of these liberals are trying to flee America, searching out greener pastures in a socialistic or a communistic country. When's the last time you saw a group of Democrats floating down to Cuba on a raft with a sail that has a big picture of Che Guevara on it?

Democrats posture as real heroes, opening gracious arms to the world's population. But so often they end up patronizing illegal immigrants because they're simply assessing them (and their patrons) as voting stock. Of course, the socialist agenda of the open-armed Democratic Party will eventually create the kind of government so many illegal immigrants were trying to get away from in the first place.

Now, as conservatives, we understand that immigration played a big role in making America the great country that she is. After all, Americans aren't better than everybody else—we *are* everybody else. It's *illegal* immigration that conservatives dislike, not immigration, and certainly not immigrants. This shouldn't even need explaining, but we are forced to explain ourselves because the liberals will try to paint us as racists, so we have to be right there with the paint thinner!

A Constitution Revolution!

I'm confident we can agree that the original Tea Party took place because citizens were tired of oppressive taxes, and without representation to boot. Today, we're tired of being taxed rotten to pay for the runaway spending of people who are misrepresenting us. Instead of being conservative with how they spend our money, they spend liberally. They deal liberally with regulations, liberally with regulatory fees, liberally with the authoring of laws, and liberally with the power of the judiciary. Liberals want the government to take on an over-all liberal size, whereas conservatives want the government to maintain a conservative size. All these liberties that the liberals take only amount to oppression.

All these liberties that the liberals take only amount to oppression.

19

So, if you're for one nation under God, and understand that this country is a constitutional republic, then you may find yourself in the Conservative Republican tent. We form a party to hold the line against a legion of selfish people hell-bent on giving themselves power through the government, taxing us into the ground in order to support their agenda.

If left wingers keep getting their way, and turn this country into their version of America, they will bring about a self-fulfilling prophecy and end up with the very America they're afraid of. I bet then they'll wish they had those second amendment rights to protect things like that first amendment they claim to uphold. For themselves, of course.

CHAPTER 3

THE FOUNDATION OF FAITH

L iberals constantly accuse me of repeating right wing propaganda I have supposedly read, and, without missing
a beat, those same liberals will say I need to read more
and get educated. Control freaks!

Liberals are always telling me *I'm* brainwashed. I get liberals
emailing me with huge lists of their resources, trying to pose
like they've done their research. All it proves to me is that they're
the ones allowing themselves to be mind-humped by a bunch of
other liberals who are just as cynical as they are.

Liberals like to present themselves as informed. You can look
right up their nose and see their memory card loaded with talking points as they stare down their nostrils at you from the top
of that high donkey they're ridin' on. And there are, of course,
the other liberals—endowed with about as much information
as a *Speak 'n' Spell*. Liberals like to read and reread the cynical
perspectives of their supposed authorities: Howard Zinn, Noam
Chomsky stuff. When I read things concerning our history, I
really prefer primary sources, not the interpretations of others.

Authors who cling to the idea that the founding fathers were
Deists fixate on particular statements, always taken out of con-
text, like this one: "The government of the United States is not

in any sense founded on the Christian Religion." Well, that's true. We're not a theocracy. Our government is not and was not a religious establishment. But the wording is very specific. The statement in question comes from the 1797 Treaty of Tripoli.

To make a long story short, there wasn't much love between the Muslims and the Christians. Big shocker. Muslims still had a grouchy grudge against the Christians for things like the Crusades and Ferdinand and Isabella's expulsion of Muslims from Granada. To avoid a high seas holy war, the treaty included words distancing the American political system from many of the European religious monarchies. This was America's attempt to appease the Muslims. It didn't work. We still had an armed conflict with the pirates... which we won.

Our government's job includes *protecting* religious establishments, not *being* a religious establishment.

22

But here's the key: the treaty didn't say, *The Constitution of the United States is not in any sense founded on the Christian Religion*. It says the *government* isn't. Our government's job includes protecting religious establishments, not *being* a religious establishment.

The Constitution itself is founded on the Judea-Christian Scripture, it is from the Scriptures that we draw the institutional separation between Church and State. Here is Scripture that shows that God does not want the government to assume religious powers:

> But when [Uzziah] became strong, his heart was so proud that he acted corruptly, and he was unfaithful to the LORD his God, for he entered the temple of the LORD to burn incense on the altar of incense. Then Azariah the priest entered after him and with him eighty priests of the LORD,

valiant men. They opposed Uzziah the king and said to him, "It is not for you, Uzziah, to burn incense to the LORD, but for the priests, the sons of Aaron who are consecrated to burn incense. Get out of the sanctuary, for you have been unfaithful and will have no honor from the LORD God."

But Uzziah, with a censer in his hand for burning incense, was enraged; and while he was enraged with the priests, the leprosy broke out on his forehead before the priests in the house of the LORD, beside the altar of incense. Azariah the chief priest and all the priests looked at him, and behold, he was leprous on his forehead; and they hurried him out of there, and he himself also hastened to get out because the LORD had smitten him. (2 Chron. 26:16–20)

God wants a government that reveres Him, yes, but He doesn't want the government to assume the role of a church and rule in His name because God knows man would rule selfishly, and invoke God's name to justify the government's abuses. *Hmmm.* That's never happened before with holy monarchies, right?

23

Only Jesus can establish the church, govern from it, and rule righteously. How did the founding fathers know this and shape the Constitution accordingly? Because the majority of them were Christians, that's how.

So, like I said, the wording of the treaty was very clever. It points out that the American *government* is not itself an arm of the Christian church or vice versa, unlike the European governments the Muslims were accustomed to fighting.

But hey, we never said anything about our Constitution, and our Constitution says, "We the people." It doesn't say, *We the government.* I understand that's not enough to satisfy the secularist. I sympathize. They don't want to believe the founders were Christian and that our Constitution is fundamentally Judeo-Christian, and people like me don't want to believe the opposite. I'm not ashamed to admit that we all gather facts to support what we desire to believe. *Facts* have little effect on the opposition because everyone has an interest in confirming what they already believe.

> *Facts* have little effect on the opposition because everyone has an interest in confirming what they already believe.

You may ask, *Well, if that's the case, and people ignore facts and are beholden to what they want to believe, then what's the point? Moreover, how does one know they're defending the right belief?* The reason I know I'm right to defend the Judeo-Christian base of our founding fathers and Constitution is because to believe the contrary would be an exercise in bitter selfishness and self-righteousness.

The founding fathers pledged their lives, fortune, and sacred honor to the defense of liberty; these were hardly selfish men. They did not exalt themselves to be accountable only to themselves. See, when those of the more Libertarian mindset use the self-righteous language of *personal* liberty and *personal* responsibility, they show they want to be accountable only to themselves. They exalt themselves as the ultimate judge of their lives; an exclusive seat reserved only for God. Doesn't the Declaration of Independence include the words, "We, therefore, the Representatives of the United States of America, in general Congress assembled, appealing to the Supreme Judge of the world. . ."? Translation: They recognized their accountability to God!

I'm not so full of myself as to assume that I know enough or that I am righteous enough to answer to myself. I am accountable to God. I believe the majority of the founding fathers were also men who humbled themselves before God, and submitted to His oversight.

The secularists don't want to be held accountable to a power beyond themselves, which (though they often don't want to admit it) ultimately gives more power to the government. But the main thing is, they don't like the idea of being judged, so they try to dismiss God as our foundation and ultimate judge. *Personal* responsibility and self-accountability are delusions, because they involve people being completely honest with themselves. Who among us has that nailed down? Maybe you're a little lax on how you conduct yourself, or you may even judge yourself too harshly.

I don't just see God as the Judge I'll answer to when I'm dead. I answer to Him *now*. My steps aren't governed by my own so-called sense of righteousness, but by His. Invoking God to give authority to one's self righteousness, which is also a manner of taking God's name in vain, plagues the world. But living by God's righteousness brings peace, joy, and prosperity. Trying to live by your own righteousness brings chaos, misery, and languishment.

I'm pretty sure some secularist is already saying, *But religion is the cause of so much chaos and suffering.* Didn't I just say that people invoke the name of God to carry out their own interests? God didn't have anything to do with that, and if God ain't in it, it ain't gonna turn out to be good.

This is why the third commandment forbids taking God's name in vain. When a person is invoking God's name to carry out his own personal interest... that's taking God's name in vain. Calling on God for the glory of your *own* cause is selfish and leads to things like slavery, genocide, and tyranny. Oh yeah, and *terrorism*. But the secularists will cling to their cynical arguments about how much suffering the God of the Bible has caused, which just isn't true. They overlook how many lives Christians have saved by bringing food, water, medicine, shelter, education, clothing.

Despite Christians being the most charitable people on Earth, secularists just parrot responses such as, *Christianity just uses charity to force Christian beliefs on others.* It wasn't the Christians causing the oppression in the first place. Christians are the ones coming with relief. Along with food, clothing, and medicine, Christians tell people where these blessings come from. God wasn't the one who afflicted them. The ungodly did. But God sent his faithful to bring relief. Of course, the big question is, *So why does God allow all this oppression in the first place?* Because people assume their righteousness is above God's. Because we trust in our rulers instead of God, and we dismiss the righteousness of God. God gives us the choice to do that. God's righteousness doesn't fail. But our choices fail to bring happiness. And sometimes, when our trust in men is broken, we finally learn to trust God's righteousness. *Sometimes.*

26

Unfortunately, true cynics maintain their prejudice against Christianity because their belief is like concrete within them. They simply *want to believe* the worst about Christianity. And these same people will try to tell you the founding fathers weren't Christian. The founding fathers risked their lives for God, and to claim their right to the gifts that only God can give: life, liberty, and the pursuit of happiness. So yeah, when they claim to be Christian, I believe them. Despite what atheists try to tell you, over ninety percent of the founding fathers were Christians. Not Deists. Here are some examples:

> O Most Glorious God, in Jesus Christ, my merciful and loving Father; I acknowledge and confess my guilt in the weak and imperfect performance of the duties of this day. I have

called on Thee for pardon and forgiveness of my sins, but
so coldly and carelessly that my prayers are become my sin,
and they stand in need of pardon.

Deists don't pray like that. George Washington was a Christian,
not a Deist.

The Gospel of Jesus Christ prescribes the wisest rules for
just conduct in every situation of life. Happy they who are
enabled to obey them in all situations!

Deists don't say that. Benjamin Rush was a Christian, not a Deist.

I have carefully examined the evidences of the Christian
religion, and if I was sitting as a juror upon its authentic-
ity I would unhesitatingly give my verdict in its favor. I can
prove its truth as clearly as any proposition ever submitted
to the mind of man.

27

Deists don't say that. Alexander Hamilton was a Christian, not
a Deist.

It cannot be emphasized too strongly or too often that this
great nation was founded, not by religionists, but by Christians; not on religions, but on the Gospel of Jesus Christ. For
this very reason peoples of other faiths have been afforded
asylum, prosperity, and freedom of worship here.

Patrick Henry was Christian, not a Deist.

Pick any founding father, and guess what? Chances are good
you're going to find he was a Christian. What? Are you going to
base your conclusion on Thomas Paine? I didn't know that he was
the final authority on what *all* the founding fathers believed. Y'all
claim to love science so much, but what kind of science arrives at
its conclusions by ignoring the majority of the evidence?

WEAPON OF A.S.S. DESTRUCTION

Go ahead and cherry pick your evidence to establish the deism of the founding fathers, but you're going to find far more evidence that the overwhelming majority were Christian. The majority of them were also *anti-slavery*. But the minority who were pro-slavery threw a big hissy fit about it, and all the rest of 'em got a bad name.

And there were those who claimed to be Christian that were pro-slavery, like Thomas Jefferson. I know you liberals know who *he* is. *Separation of church and state! Thomas Jefferson said so!* I agree with him! And by the way, Thomas Jefferson was a self-proclaimed Christian:

> To the corruptions of Christianity, I am indeed opposed; but not to the genuine precepts of Jesus Himself. I am a Christian, in the only sense in which He wished anyone to be.

28 So, according to Jefferson, he was a Christian.

Ha! You are so busted, Zo! Jefferson was a Christian, but he was a Christian who supported slavery. See! You Christians just want everyone to be slaves.

And again, Liberals want to look exclusively at that instance which supports their agenda while ignoring the majority of instances where Christians rose up to fight slavery. These Christians gave their lives because Jesus Christ is the truth, and this truth sets men free. So, if we really are the followers of Christ, then we have a duty to set men free from the liars who tell them they aren't worthy of freedom.

And these Christian men did, even if some of them thought of blacks as an inferior race. They still acknowledged their humanity, and bled for their freedom when the Civil War came. The point here is to illustrate a few more instances on how the left is hoodwinking you.

To Christian Democrats, let me say a few things:

The very people in your party insult you and the God you believe in, and are able to do it because they've kept you prejudiced against Republicans. You're so conditioned to believe Republicans are racists that you overlook the racist and God-despising Democrats you remain loyal to. This is just another instance of not seeing the forest through the trees. The liberal establishment is not interested in your advancement. They're interested in your dependency. That translates into *power* for them.

> The liberal establishment is not interested in your advancement. They're interested in your dependency.

Now, even though there are liberal Republicans, I'm not one of those people who says, *I've had it with Republicans! I'm leaving.* I'm the kind that establishes what it means to be a Republican. And you're not taking that away from us.

Liberalism is a disease that infects both parties, and the Bible is the elixir. It's the medicine that is more accepted by the Republican body because the disease of liberalism has progressed too far in the Democratic body. So, I'll gladly stick with being a conservative Republican. But there are a lot of Republicans in serious need of a booster shot.

Movin' on, the thing about the entitlement culture of liberal Democrats is that they are concerned only with what they can get from the system. The system that they hate, mind you. Yet the system they hate is the very system they create! They, along with the elitist liberal Democrats who patronize them, are leading us deeper into socialism. How did this happen?

How is it that Conservatives have to keep struggling against liberals? The liberal ideology is so deficient in redeeming value, y'all. We should be able to dropkick liberalism into the land of missing sock-mates. It's as if they sold their souls to the Devil to be able to beat us with nothing. The celebration of the equal sharing of misery is about all liberalism gives people to look forward to. And the promises of career liberals cost way more than the promised benefits are worth.

They lead a fist-pumping festival against the Republicans, the corporations, the military, the church, and America. *Hey, hey, ho, ho! [Fill in the blank] has got to go!*

Conservatism works. Even liberals know that. That's why liberals are trying to lay claim to our language. For example, they'll say: *Democrats are the real conservatives, we conserve jobs, the environment, the economy, etc.*

Liberalism has a more effective delivery system, but the liberal idea is not the more practical application. Liberalism is delivered with laser shows; gorgeous, busty women; handsome (sexual orientation unknown) men; gratuitous profanity; karate choppin' movies; big, cute, fuzzy-wuzzy polar bears; superheroes; gourmet coffee; tattoos; booty shakin' music; fart jokes; etc.

Of course, I'm not suggesting *we* should resort to cheap tricks. (Fart jokes are funny though.) But the conservative message has the stigma of being delivered by stuffy, rich, white males. Rush Limbaugh comes to mind, but I don't think Rush is stuffy. God has anointed Rush with so much cool that if the ice caps were truly melting away, Rush could visit them, tell 'em to chill, and it would be so.

30

Liberals are very prejudiced. Prejudice is easy and contagious. Liberals have commanded how conservatives are to be portrayed, and are beating right wingers half to death with their own stereotypical golf clubs. As well as being prejudiced, liberals are very superficial. They're interested in what looks good and feels good, but not in what *is* good.

(It must be added that being prejudiced and angry also feels good to liberals. They love feeling justified and passionate as they revel in their own righteousness, ranting against what they feel is wrong.)

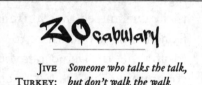

JIVE
TURKEY: *Someone who talks the talk, but don't walk the walk*

They apply whatever intellect they have to argue for immorality, dependency, and things that are impractical... and they can be very creative about it. People can be very persuasive when selfishness is the engine of their argument. Liberals are totally self-serving, but they convince themselves (and others) that they're acting in the community's interest. And just a reminder, liberalism infects Republicans as well as Democrats. Too many Republicans assume office as eagles, and then turn out to be jive turkeys!

31

But liberal Democrats take the cake. They put more energy into sucking money from workers and businesses to promote prejudice against Republicans than they do into helping the people they claim to care so much about. That's right. As much as they claim to care about the less fortunate, they spend far more time, money and effort in spreading hatred for the right wing. This is what's truly more important to liberals than spreading the wealth to the people they claim to advocate.

Republicans get accused of being power-hungry and wanting to control the masses, yet it's the liberal Democrats who dominate the most powerful and influential occupations. They dominate the academic arena, indoctrinating instead of educating. They dominate the media—conducting America's mood and perspective. They dominate the entertainment industry—shaping our culture. They dominate the activist judicial system—legislating when they should be adjudicating. It is liberals that hold the lion's share of power and influence. Not conservatives.

If you're living in a city with high crime and low employment, high incarceration rates and few high school graduates, it is virtually guaranteed that you're in a city that is run by Democrats. Don't blame Republicans. You hate them and don't vote them in to office. It's the Democrats you keep voting in that screw up your community. The "establishment" that liberals at the lower end of the totem pole hate so much is just more liberals at the higher end of the totem pole. How do these elitist liberals stay there?

"The Man" is a liberal. "The Establishment" is liberal. The system liberals hate *is* liberalism.

They stay there by accusing Republicans of oppressing the underdog, by accusing republicans of being fat cats who don't care about the little guy. While the biggest fat cats are your Democratic union bosses. Liberals promote class warfare to keep the "have-nots" from attacking the upper class liberals, leaving the elitist liberal establishment to reign. Face it. "The Man" is a liberal. "The Establishment" is liberal. The system liberals hate *is* liberalism.

Conservative Republicans are accused of being power-hungry. If we were so hungry for power, we would do the things that would give us this so-called power. We would make pandering our main strategy, since power comes from votes. We would say *yes* to abortion to appeal to feminist voters. We would say *yes* to open borders to attract the Hispanic vote. *Yes* to gay marriage to attract the homosexual vote. *Yes* to rejecting God to attract the secularist vote. *Yes* to reparations and affirmative action to attract the black vote. *Yes* to welfare to attract the entitlement-minded vote. Democrats do say *yes* to these things because they want the votes for the sake of power, and with that power they do nothing but oppress the very people who gave them that power while encouraging bitter prejudice against the Republican Party.

At this point some people ask, *Well, what is the Republican Party going to do for me?* The Republican Party is about conserving your freedoms to *do for yourself.* Republicans aren't looking to do for you; that would make you dependent on them. And remember, you can't be dependent on someone without allowing them to control you. Democrats want to control you.

You liberals are always saying we need to do more for others. Well, get a job and do something for somebody, then. And, if you have a job, quit complaining about doing things for people. That's the way to be of service to others. But entitlement-minded liberals don't want to help others. A lot of liberals resent having to be of service to customers, and they resent making money for some rich guy. If liberals really had a servant's heart, that wouldn't be an issue. Providing a service would be their pleasure, and they would learn how to run a business so they could be of more service to others. But instead, they would rather put that energy into resenting their job—and the job creator.

Anyway, liberals are right to believe there is an oppressor, an enemy, or "The Man," but it ain't the conservatives, it's elitist liberal Democrats—wolves in sheeple's clothing. You can find people screwing up and screwing people over on both sides of the aisle. But, it's normal with Democrats. It's so normal, people

33

don't notice it. With Republicans, it can stick out. That's why it's such a big deal. It's like a straight-A student getting a D in P.E.

I'm a Christian conservative Republican patriot based on the following:

I'm a *Christian* because I understand that God's righteousness is infinitely better than ours. No matter how many supposed flaws the Bible bashers think they can find with God, not one on this earth is more righteous than He. These elitist non-believers can't grasp that because they believe there is nothing higher than humans. Yet, at the same time, they feel there's nothing *lower* than humans. And, of course, they don't include *themselves* in the denominator of the human equation.

I'm a *conservative* because I understand that freedom is a gift from God. Gifts from God have great power, and freedom is no exception. As the saying goes, "With great power comes great responsibility."

I'm a *Republican* because I understand we enjoy a constitutional republic, not a democracy. Democrats keep trying to say this is a Democracy. It's good marketing. Democracy sounds good, but it goes bad. Democracy means the majority rules. Majority rule is based upon what is popular; which means that the very nature of Democrats is to vote for what's *popular* over what's *right*.

The very nature of democracy is to vote for what's *popular* over what's *right*.

I'm a *patriot* because I live in a country where I'm free to love the God who blessed us with freedom. Democrats are trying to take that away from us. They keep complaining that we're try-

34

ing to push our God on them, but they want to force atheism on the country. Total hypocrites.

I'm a capitalist because the Constitution does not list income taxes as a means for Congress to collect revenue. If I worked to earn it, it's mine to spend. When we're able to keep more money we're able to spend more on charities, tithe, and paying wages. We're able to buy more products and services and sell them for lower prices. So the introduction of the liberal Sixteenth Amendment can suck it. Actually, that's exactly what it does. It's a life-sucking amendment.

I support the Second Amendment because it is our last resort to protect our Constitution in the event the First Amendment is no longer effective.

When it comes to immigration, all are welcome to this country who enter legally and pull their weight, as long as they don't try to turn this country into the socialist or communist country they just risked their lives to leave.

35

When it comes to unborn children, a child in the womb's right to live overrides a woman's "choice" to terminate the life she carries. There is no instance that puts the child at fault—there is no reason for the child to pay the death penalty.

When it comes to your retirement savings, it should be whatever you've paid into it. You shouldn't force others to pay into it, and you shouldn't be forced to pay for someone else's retirement.

The founding fathers wanted education to be available to all children because the founding fathers wanted everybody to know how to read. Why? Because they wanted them to be free to read the Bible. Education should be available to everybody, but it should not be and wasn't meant to be facilitated by income taxes. People should have the right to keep the money they earn and put it towards the school they see fit to send their child to.

Now because I have views such as these, I'm heartless. It's said that conservatives are only conservative when it comes to helping the poor. That's cute. A more accurate statement would be conservatives are only conservative about helping people who are conservative about helping themselves, unless they're *helping themselves* to the fruits of someone else's earnings. Yeah, I'm quite sure that's a more accurate way of putting it.

CHAPTER 4

RIGHT WING FAITH, LEFT WING FANTASY

'm black. You know that and I know that, but there are many who insist I'm not. According to the Afrocentrics and those who patronize them, I'm whitewashed. It's funny when I've got liberal, white people trying to tell me they're blacker than I am. Wow! How is it that white people trying to be black can accuse me of trying to be white? That's some hypocrisy that's just too funny! They're taking blind shots, hoping to get a nod from the black community to sedate their white guilt.

Don't you love it when white liberals insult anybody white, male, and heterosexual, feeling like they get a pass because, after all, they claim to fight for minorities? These white liberals do not intend to legitimately help these minorities, they just don't want those minorities to turn against them.

So, the only thing these white, liberal democrats (the true white devils, mind you) do for the so-called minorities is pander. Liberals manipulate many non-whites and women with one simple tool—the tool that can turn even loved ones against you. The very tool that changed Adam and Eve's perception of God—a deadly tool—*accusation*.

THE ACCUSER

The very name *Satan* does not translate to mean *Evil One*, *Deceiver*, *Prince of Darkness*, or even *Tempter*. His name literally means *Accuser*.

When Satan spoke with Eve, he accused God of not wanting them to eat from the tree of knowledge of good and evil because God didn't want them to be like God. That was the statement that broke Eve. That was what damaged the relationship between God and humanity.

Satan's accusation made it sound like God was trying to keep Adam and Eve down, doesn't it? This caused Eve to be envious of God and to distrust Him. Satan made it look like God was holding out and hoarding power—it made it look like He had arrested humanity's development.

38

What if we apply that truth to our political situation? *The Republicans are just trying to arrest the development of the black community. They don't care about blacks, or women, blah, blah, yap, yap, etc.* It's fitting that women would be easily manipulated by liberalism because Satan, the biggest liberal of them all, went to Eve first, and manipulated her by causing her to not trust another male figure. Just like Adam and Eve trusted the accuser who wanted them destroyed, the majority of minorities—the black community, Hispanics, women, and secular Jews—trust the party that would see them destroyed.

So check this out. Before Lucifer became the Accuser, he was God's most anointed cherub. Now, just as there was a Civil War because Democrats didn't see blacks as worthy to be considered human, God's most anointed cherub did not see humans as worthy of the position for which God created us.

As Lucifer became Satan, he formed a confederacy. He used accusations and discourse such as, *God wants only to control us! We should be allowed to live out our own destiny, outside of His design! God has this idea of humans having authority in our society. What about our authority? What about our great society that God wants to stain with these humans by bringing them into existence with us? We're superior. They have no place among us! They're not fit to even look on us!*

Man, what a hater!

These accusations rallied a third of the angels behind the rebellious cherub, and he led an attempted coup against the Throne. He fell, and (as is typical of Satan) he used another accusation to bring a curse upon humankind in Eden. That curse still affects us, and the Democrats have learned to manipulate this weakness. "You shall not bear false witness against your neighbor" is a command the Democrats depend on breaking in order to gain power. They do just as the Accuser does.

39

Now, Satan didn't (and still doesn't) know how good he had it, crying about oppression in heaven. Liberals are the same way today—crying about oppression in America. Hey, wanna have some fun? Ask some liberals why they're Democrats. Chances are real good that the first thing they'll give you is an accusation. *I'm a Democrat because the corporations are corrupt, and because republicans are destroying the earth. They are against equal rights! They are bigoted, sexist homophobes, rabble, rabble, rabble.*

Hey! Liberal! I didn't ask you why you're *not* a Republican. I asked why you *are* a Democrat. Accusations made by Democrats encourage prejudice and animosity against Republicans— the people that fought for the freedom of blacks and the equality of women. What have Republicans gotten in return? Hatred.

Unjustly Accused

Liberals fan the fire with questions like, *What are Republicans gonna do for blacks? How come Republicans don't come to the inner cities and help?* (Um, because people in the inner cities hate Republicans. That's why.) Liberals curse, threaten, and intimidate Republicans, making sure their community is a place where angels fear to tread.

But then people get mad because Republicans aren't coming to the rescue! Weird, man!

The reason there aren't that many non-whites in the Republican Party isn't because they're not welcome, it's because liberals and Democrats ridicule and threaten people who are even thinking about going Republican, making people believe the Republicans want only whites in their party.

40

But, on the other hand, Republicans gotta take some responsibility too. Republicans don't make their presence known very well, which gives liberals more leverage with which to influence people. Republicans don't want all the drama of people being in their face, accusing them of stuff they haven't done. All the while, these people continue voting for the party responsible for their mistreatment. I understand. But I'm sorry, Republicans, there are always going to be people who are going to have to bear what seems to be an unfair and unreasonable burden.

How can we talk about how much we admire our soldiers who are prepared to run into battle while we shrink at the burden of trying to connect with the understandably abrasive victims of Democratic malevolence? How do we dare talk about the bravery of our troops who are ready to give all, while, at the same time, we're too afraid to say we're conservative because some liberal might get mad at us? You're afraid you might lose your *job?* We stand to lose our *country.* And trust me, we *will* lose it if we don't stand up to these liberals right now. Your career ain't gonna mean much if we lose the country to liberal schemin'. Think about how hard it must have been for abolitionist Republicans to say, *I support freedom for blacks.* Democrats lynched white Republicans for vocally supporting abolition. There was a time when Republicans lost their lives for being Republicans—and were willing to do

> **Are you afraid you might lose your *job?* We stand to lose our *country.***

so. Are you made of the same stuff as those Republicans? Or are you okay with tip-toeing around Democrats? You think it's hard finding work now? It's getting harder, isn't it? We've got to take a stand against these liberals now, 'cause it's only going to get worse if we don't.

41

We've got to let folks know that we've got a rose garden of capitalism, yet the weeds of socialism are growin' and chokin' our economy. Unfortunately, Republicans haven't been breakin' out with the weed-eater. They're not getting the message to the folks in the hearts of the cities. Those places badly need to hear truths like, *You're not going to benefit from punishing the job creators. Feeling good about a rich person getting punished isn't going to pay your rent, and it certainly isn't going to make it cheaper.*

I've heard liberals ask, *What has a Republican ever done for you?* Well, we Republicans aren't hung up on people *doing* for us. We can do for ourselves. We help those who put more effort into making progress rather than making excuses. We help those who carry their own weight instead of carrying a chip on their shoulder.

Conservatives know there are people needin' a hand up, but living off of handouts is just triflin'. It's all about a hand *up*, not a hand*out*.

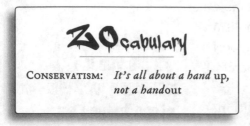

CONSERVATISM: *It's all about a hand* up, *not a hand*out

Also, let's not put more faith in politicians than we do in the Almighty. Liberals depend on some politicians to come and change things for them, when the change they need can be made by only themselves—that change is to realize that God is the way, and that He has equipped them to make their lives better.

It's harder for some than others, I know. There are some who make it very difficult for others to live free. When there are people with any power ignoring or misinterpreting God's Word, then the people under that person's control suffer. It's not God making them suffer, it's the leader's actions due to the disregard of God's benevolent laws or the malevolent interpretation and execution of His laws. Many ask, *Why does God allow all the suffering in the world?* Because *we* do. He gives us authority as to what we allow into the world, and we have to deal with that. It's our responsibility.

Every one of us, to some degree, bring something into the world that is not good. Falsely accusing, or stealing, or cheating, or coveting—these things affect other people, and we have to deal with what we have allowed into the world. We gave entrance to what brings us suffering, not God. God gave the warning, and the warning was ignored. Now we have to deal with what we allowed into the world; but God will help us deal. Instead of questioning why God allows suffering, we'd do better to follow His instructions for preventing problems and knowing how to

42

best deal with problems when they arise. He's blessed us with the skills to solve and prevent problems.

People accuse God of not answering them, but I wonder if they considered that they're not answering God. People try to deal with life by their own righteousness. This only makes the world more chaotic. God's righteousness is the formula for peace, joy, and prosperity.

Instead of questioning why God allows suffering, we'd do better to follow His instructions for preventing it.

CHAPTER 5

THE CASE FOR CAPITALISM

'm going to say it up front: capitalism without faith in God becomes *crapitalism*. Without Christ, we end up with people buying things that shouldn't be sold and other people selling things that shouldn't be bought.

But I wouldn't tell you what you can or cannot buy or sell (like the State does). I just wouldn't buy your products—I would boycott. Boycotting is the *people* saying no to your business, not the State, so it's not censorship.

Capitalism is often mistaken for opportunism, or just flat-out greed and corruption. Capitalism really has nothing to do with either. Capitalism

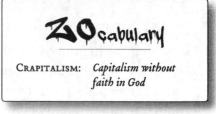

ZOcabulary

CRAPITALISM: *Capitalism without faith in God*

makes for the most honest economic system. All capitalism means is that the government cannot claim our income. *That's all*. Your capital is *your* capital. However, in socialistic, communistic, or (like we have) crony capitalism, there *are* more reasons for businessmen to be dishonest with their earnings. So-called government oversight is just another means and excuse for the government to impose higher punitive taxes and regulatory fees.

Then people often resort to crime to recover the cost of what the government takes. People have a somewhat understandable reason to engage in corruption in such economies. Capitalism minimizes such draw to corruption. Capitalism isn't hiding money from the government like these criminals are. In a capitalist system, you don't feel the need to hide your wealth because the government doesn't have the power to take it from you.

See, when people are oppressed, maintaining an oppressed mindstate, they are easily coerced into socialism or communism. Look at the Jews. Their Holocaust was brought upon them by the socialist Nazi party. Yet today, most of the Jews in America support the socialist policies of Democrats. And look at the black community. Oppressed by Democrats throughout our early history, today the black community supports the socialist policies of Democrats. Whether it's Russia, China, or Mexico, there is an invasion of socialistic and communistic sentiment in America. Now I'm talking about a mindset. Not *people*. Don't get it twisted. It's the *policies* of these countries I'm against—not their *people*.

Crony capitalism, brought on by the liberal government and beholden to the unions, is bleeding our economy. The union bosses are rich elitists who are doing the people dirty, yet liberals don't complain about them. Remember, Hitler, Mao, Stalin, Lenin, Mussolini, and Pol Pot were anti-capitalist and were pro-government oversight.

THE ROOT OF ALL EVIL?

The Bible says that the love of money is the root of all evil. Keep in mind that the *love* of money is the root of all evil, not the money itself. If money were evil, God would not accept it as a tithe! Therefore, it is not evil for you to have money. It's not evil for you to have a lot of money. It's evil for you to love your money.

Whether you only have a little bit of money or a whole lot of money, it's evil for you to love any of it.

In a capitalist system, you don't feel the need to hide your wealth because the government doesn't have the power to take it from you.

What's also evil is being selfish. And loving money tends to cause people to be very selfish. But not so fast, my entitlement-minded, socialist, liberal friend. You're probably agreeing and saying, *That's right, the rich shouldn't be so selfish*, expecting them to give some of that money to you. Well, it's also evil to covet. It's one of God's top ten no-no's. It's *not* one of God's Ten Commandments that the rich has to give money to the poor; but it is one of God's Ten Commandments that you do not covet the belongings of someone else.

Of course, a lot of liberals will say, *Hey, I don't believe in your God anyway*. And others will try to twist the Scripture to fit their entitlement-minded selfishness. And as they selectively believe in whatever parts of the Bible suit them, they'll pick out still other Scriptures and twist them to vilify capitalism.

47

THE HAVE- AND HAVE-NOT-YETS

There are many people who act like the state of the *have* and *have-nots* began with America. There have always been the *have* and the *have-nots*—long before America. The truth is, no country has done a better job of creating more opportunities for the *have-nots* to work their way out of poverty and thrive. Capitalism makes for more jobs and leaves people with more money to be charitable. The *only* reason why charity wouldn't be as prominent would be that those needing charity would already have jobs because the job creator could afford to hire.

Unfortunately, what keeps a lot of people out of a job these days is people thinking they're entitled to a *job*, but not actually wanting to *work*. They want to come to work dressed like it's Halloween with all their piercings and weird hairdos, and they expect the managers and the customers to just accept it: *I'm an individual, so you have to accept my individuality.*

Uh... no, I don't. And not only that, but you gotta earn individuality. Then, after you pay your dues, you can leave the workplace and go play individually all you want. Don't get me wrong—I'm all about individuality. But one's individuality shouldn't come at the expense of others. I know a lot of you young liberals want to be an individual on your own terms. It doesn't work that way. You got to be an individual on your own dime.

The entitlement-minded aren't ready for real work. They have their mindset on how they want to live, and as far as they're concerned, you owe it to them.

48

This kind of mindset supports socialism and communism. Liberals think that charity, social responsibility, socialism, and communism are all the same, utopian thing. They don't realize that the very thing they claim to hate is the very thing they demand: fascism. They have no idea what real charity is. When the government takes money from you to give to someone else, that's not charity. It's *theft*.

> **When the government takes money from you to give to someone else, that's not charity. It's *theft*.**

For you liberals out there that say Jesus was a socialist: Nope. Jesus wanted people to give from their *heart*. That's charity. Having the government force money from you to give to someone else does not impress Jesus.

CAPITALISM IS FREEDOM OF MONEY

Capitalism isn't about how much money you can make. Capitalism is about you being able to use what you make in the way you see fit, without the government taking whatever it wants. Capitalists believe in self-reliance. Socialists believe in forced social reliance, and communists believe in total government reliance. When you are self-reliant, you are independent. You depend on *you*. If you are socially reliant, you are dependent on society to relinquish a portion of their earnings to the government for your use.

Communists think the government should be the people's sole provider, which is merely totalitarianism. Workers work to satisfy only the State. They think of prosperity as shared by the people, but this so-called prosperity is distributed by State design. Communists want the establishment of a classless society, but that takes a heavy-handed government. You can't get away from the State on that one.

49

In socialism and communism, the illusion is that they're all working for each other. But these economies collapse because so many people are waiting to *take* advantage of the fruits of other people's labor. And they're dependent on the State to take more and more in the hopes that they'll get to enjoy what's been taken from the few remaining hard workers. It's a culture of careless dependency.

As a self-reliant capitalist, you are dependent on people only to pay voluntarily for a product or service you provide. If you are a government-reliant socialist, you are dependent on other people's income to provide for your comforts. If you are a wealthy socialist, you try to dodge condemnation by patronizing those who aren't wealthy. This is often done by attacking others who are wealthy so that the poor will take their hateful focus off of you and accept you as one of *them*.

For example, people like Michael Moore and union bosses are socialist elitists. Socialism and fascism go hand in hand, adding to control, and the socialist/fascist elite want to control the people—those unwittingly controlled people who are loyal to the patronizing elitists. They are promised entitlements, which in turn keep them tolerant of their barely satisfactory life, eventually pacifying their angst by stoking their animosity toward job creators. The hypocritical wealthy socialist elitists provoke them to vent their anger against the job creators because it keeps them controlled—and voting Democrat. Just give them someone else to blame, and you've made a friend.

If you are a government-dependent communist, then you fully submit to government control for government provisions. I know, I know. You think you're doing it for the people. Well, sorry. You're doing it for the State. The people will have little reason to better themselves. You exist to feed the State, and the State will feed you *just enough* to keep you feeding the State *more than enough*. The State will encourage excellence so that you aren't a burden on the system, but you certainly won't enjoy excellence in return.

In a free market, you get to enjoy your excellence and are free to utilize it. The only people who criticize commercialization are envious people who covet the success of others and become sour and cynical.

Free market capitalists have nobody to blame but themselves should they fail, no matter how big they get. This is why liberals reject the idea of being capitalist. They can't take blame, remember? They don't have the spine for it, and being that they are socialist, and communist minded, they are dependent on society, or government, to bear the weight of their failures.

Crony capitalism is the Frankenstein's monster that liberals hate, but have created. Liberals like to say all capitalism is crony capitalism, but this isn't true. Like I said, capitalism is when you keep the fruits of your labor. The government cannot claim your income. Now, regulations and legislations are legitimate, but the government may not lay claim to your capital. Crony capitalism, however, is simply socialism *funded* by capitalism. For example, a socialist State owns industry. In crony capitalism, the industry isn't owned by the State per se, but the State takes money from people to subsidize their pet industries. Crony capital-ism can also be seen in the form of unions. Unions are collection firms, pulling in revenue for the Democratic Party. The unions pressure, sometimes force, people to join, then use their dues to juice the DNC.

VOcabulary

CRONY   *Socialism funded by*
CAPITALISM: *capitalism*

51

Unions demand outrageous compensation packages for people with no vocational skills, and this forces employers to raise prices in order to recover their cost.

So, when you go the grocery store and you're wondering why food is so expensive, thank liberal Democrats and unions, because now you know the reason you can barely afford your grocery bills. They demand more money than what their service is actually worth, and as their demands are met and they live comfortably, you're going broke.

Just stop and ask yourself for a moment—what is it about union workers that they can't make do without the things you and I make do without? Don't let Democrats and unions trick you into believing they're victims. They're conniving bullies, and the truth is, they're running a game on you. If life is so much better working for unions, why are these miserable people always going on strike?

Capitalism is the most natural economic system. Why? Because it is based on what everybody, even liberals, claim to be: individuals. It's a tool that gives incentive to make you better at what you were called to do. It grates on my nerves when liberals say, *We shouldn't have a one-size-fits-all system.* They don't understand that socialism and communism are one-size-fits-all suits that don't suit our nature as individuals. Capitalism *is* the customizable suit that naturally adapts to whoever wears it, and the people who fight the hardest against this are liberal Democrats!

American liberals are so committed to driving themselves into the very things they claim to be against. They think they're so cool for demanding socialism and want someone like Che Guevara to be their leader. I saw a bulletin with Che Guevara on it with the words "Think Differently." Che was a hate-filled communistic atheist who imprisoned and murdered people for thinking outside his box.

52

Capitalism is a win-win system. Self-reliance and strong individualism are the elements of a stronger whole. We can help each other when our own circumstances are secure. We can endure hard times better because we've practiced being resourceful. Should you need someone else's help, it will be more feasible because the person you need help from hasn't had their resources sucked away by social parasites.

Democrats call themselves the party of the working class, yet those able-bodied, able-minded people who *could* work, but instead live off of government assistance, vote Democratic. You're not going to find too many Republican voters living off of welfare.

For every CEO who might be getting government money under the table, there are a thousand Democratic voters waiting for the first and the fifteenth to roll around, so they can get paid to keep doing nothing.

I am a proponent of the excise tax because it is constitutional. It's a win-win scenario when people are allowed to keep the fruits of their labor. My first fruits go to God, not the government. When people are allowed to keep their money, they will spend it. The more they spend, the more the government gets in excises. Wow, so simple! The excise tax should be a maximum of ten percent. God doesn't even ask for a specific amount over ten percent.

Now, don't tell me that what I'm suggestin' is a pipe dream. America itself was a pipe dream, yet here we are. This book ain't for naysayers. Are you an American't or an American?

ZO-CONOMICS

Do you think these economic scholars have done a fantastic job with our money? Looks to me like they've done no more than make things very complicated. Let's try some simplicity. I suggest the cities give ten percent of their take from commerce to their county. The counties then take ten percent of what they got from the cities, and give it to their state.

Then states give ten percent of what they got from the counties to the federal government. Think of all the sales tax revenue that the cities will gain from people who are spending because they're allowed to keep their earnings!

Think of all the tax revenue the counties, states, and country will gain when they collect ten percent from all the cities, counties, and states, with their own ninety percent left over to put back into their own county, city, and citizens!

Now, I'm not talking about special excise taxes. It would be general and uniform; anything that would be sold for the first time would be taxed right there. Also, to those who would say that this would just amount to being a Value Added Tax: that's fine with me. I'll take that any day with the repeal of the Sixteenth Amendment. Junk the income tax, and yeah, I'll take the VAT tax.

VALUE ADDED TAX:	*A consumption tax system in which the mark-up of goods is taxed—the value added*

The civil government's job is to protect the God-given rights to life, liberty, the pursuit of happiness, and property. Our Constitution was written to keep the people protected from its very protectors. See, people go into office not quite understanding that it's their job to protect us. They go in thinking it's the role of government to provide for us. And, for them, that turns into *controlling* us.

54

The government is constantly violating our God-given right to property with income taxes, and the president at that point should be stepping in and saying, *Hey, Congress, you are in violation of the people's right to property. Get your hands out of the people's pocket!*

Now, I don't think I have to tell you that I believe that the Sixteenth Amendment should be repealed. It is totally unconstitutional because it violates the people's right to their property. I'd rather be accused of *oversimplifying* things than *overcomplicating* them.

The IRS may not like this idea because it would put them out of business. Actually, I think they would still be needed, but now their job would be geared towards taking money from the local, state, and federal government, instead of taking money from you! The job of the IRS would be to police the government and make sure the local, state, and federal government collects and relinquishes their ten percent.

If the government really wants to stimulate the economy, they could start by stopping taxes on labor and business and tax only purchases. When a business pays for materials, they pay ten percent sales tax. When they pay their employees, they pay a ten percent sales tax because they're buying that person's time and service.

I know it's lofty. One obstacle is that the left will just call it capitalistic greed, as if greed doesn't exist in socialism and communism—as if money is loved by only the rich and not by the poor. Many people love what they don't have and can get desperate enough to do something unlawful to get it. Don't try to blame the rich for this. The rich are the ones providing jobs that give a person a way out of poverty.

55

Liberals hurt people the most by making business owners out to be boogiemen. It's not a business owner's job to get you out of poverty, but, by giving you a job, they're giving you an opportunity to sustain *yourself* and make your own way out of poverty. To those who insist businesses are corrupt: is it really going to help to put the government in charge of everything? Who lied and told you there is less corruption in the government than in business?

Who lied and told you there is less corruption in government than in business?

Throughout history, all genocidal campaigns in which people were killed by the millions have been done by governments, not by corporations. Okay, okay, I'll concede one corporation: Planned Parenthood. That corporation has killed millions upon millions. Oh, but wait. These are a bunch of socialist- and communist-minded liberals. But what about the cigarette corporations? They kill people too! Well, not really. People may use cigarettes to kill themselves, but the cigarette companies don't make them smoke. I don't care how good their advertisement campaigns are. An unborn child, however, doesn't volunteer to be killed.

Planned Parenthood is a corporation that kills, and it does so with money that the government takes from people. So, who lied to you and told you there's not as much corruption in the government? Don't answer that. I already know. I'm just not sure if you socialists and communists have thought this through. Greed is just as prevalent in socialism and communism as capitalism, if not more so.

56

But you can't expect a family-supporting wage in exchange for doing work that typically takes little skill. Don't be mad at Walmart because they don't pay their employees what an attorney makes every hour. The unions and Democrats promote a prejudice that Walmart is so horrible to its employees. If Walmart is so awful, why do people flock to Walmart for jobs? If Walmart is so awful, why do the unions want to force Walmart to employ them? And since Walmart refuses to unionize, the unions, like spoiled children, want to destroy Walmart. If *we* can't work there, *nobody* can.

If unions take over Walmart, then Walmart will not be able to give customers savings because the prices will be raised in order to pay the selfish union workers. Democrats prohibit cities from constructing Walmarts within city limits—which denies construction jobs. A lot of construction workers are in unions, but they hate Walmart more than they want the work. The unions and Democrats have tried to get people to hate Walmart by making people believe Walmart runs out mom-and-pop shops, but more often Walmart brings them more traffic. There are many small businesses that aren't threatened by Walmart, like dry cleaners, restaurants, and martial arts studios.

The point I'm trying to make here is that if you want to make more money then learn a skill that's in demand. Don't whine about how you don't have the time or a sitter or how hard it is to enroll. You can waste your time crying about how hard it is to get into a class or get the money to learn a skill or how life sucks, or you can suck it up and go get a skill.

Either way, it's going to be hard. But one of those hard roads leads out of poverty.

Minimum Wage Takes More than It Gives

57

Minimum wage is a joke, and it's a vicious cycle that only makes the prices of products go up. If the government forces a company to continue increasing how much they have to pay employees, then that company has to raise the price of their products in order to be able to make the money to pay the new wage. Which means that, while the minimum wage earner may be all happy that the boss has to pay more, the minimum wage earner will start to notice that his or her new wage isn't going that far. Funny, it seems like whenever he wants to spend that extra money, things seem to have gotten a little more expensive. Gee, I wonder why that happened! Now we are back to square one and the same people are saying we need an increase in minimum wage.

People have been duped into thinking that, if there isn't a minimum wage, then people would be working for free. Well, you have to bear in mind that a business needs employees to make or sell products to make money. This makes the employees important to that business, and, if you are important, then you will be paid depending on what your task and skills are worth.

MINIMUM WAGE:	*A tool the government uses to simultaneously raise pay rates and the price of goods*

Of course, the employer is going to want to pay the least amount possible. *You will too.* I'll prove it to you. When you go to the store, you look for bargains, don't you? I doubt you go to the store looking for the most expensive items you can find. However, if you *are* looking to spend more money, it's because you're expecting a higher quality to show for it. It's the same way with hiring employees. If an employee is a quality worker, then an employer will want to keep that person working there and will try to pay that worker more to motivate him to stay.

58

So think about it. Why is it okay for you to look for the cheapest deal, but if an employer does the same thing, they're greedy scrooges.

An employer is not going to find someone to work for them for free. The employer will have to consider the minimum cost to live and will have to be able to pay that cost to get people interested in seeking employment there. Nobody is going to put up a sign that says, *Come work for me for free.* As an employee, are you going to go to a business to offer your services for free? No, you expect them to pay you for your work.

The mandate for people to pay freed slaves a living wage was the precursor to the minimum wage that the Democrats have now co-opted as a voter attraction tool. I'm sure you've heard it before: *If I'm elected I will fight to raise the minimum wage.* The voters are enticed by that, and there you go. The minimum wage is rooted in reconstruction, which was advanced by Republicans and twisted by liberal Democrats.

DON'T UNIONIZE

Unions drive up the cost of living because they demand such extravagant compensation packages. The unions were necessary once upon a time. They stood up for the fair treatment of workers. It is true that business owners in too many cases made employees work long and then paid them short. They'd make them work in unsafe conditions, knowing that the employee would do it because they needed the money.

It's absolutely disgusting how employees were exploited. Unions are a force that helped change that. The Irish were already seen as the white ni**ers and were doing back-breaking work in the mines and on the railroads. If anybody was going to be paid it might as well be them. They may be Catholic but at least they're not black. Sometimes even being white wasn't enough when it came to the Irish, though, because they had to deal with discriminatory signs that said "No Irish Need Apply."

59

Things like those are the reasons why we have labor unions in America. But the unions themselves became racist as the Democrats found their way in and relied on bigoted sentiments, keeping the jobs for whites and narrowing the competition for jobs. So began the marriage of the unions and the Democratic Party, for the unions could rely on the Democrats for legislation like the racist Anti-Coolie Act.

The bottom line is that unions were formed because of the unfair treatment of workers. It was a noble effort that was soon corrupted by greed, bigotry, and the Democratic Party. Democrats hated the Irish, and now the Democrats have taken over what the Irish helped establish in America. But that's what Democrats do. They co-opt things that were meant for good and twist them into voter attraction tools.

Unions are just a big nuisance now—and infested with thugs. They act as if being in the union is so great, yet they're always striking because they're miserable and greedy, and there's no use in trying to satisfy them. Liberals are always talking about the greedy rich, but they don't say anything about the greediest of the rich: the union bosses. Unions demand more compensation than their service is worth, and the consumer pays the difference.

Or, in the case of teachers, they demand to be paid even when it's apparent that they're doing a lousy job. They're too stubborn and self-righteous to face the reality that they are failures at being educators. It's like telling a really bad mother she's a really bad mother. She will have a fit. She will be more upset than if you tell a good mother she's a bad mother. But facing the truth is a sword that cuts deep, and it's something that she will most likely take with great bitterness.

> Unions demand more compensation than their service is worth, and the consumer pays the difference.

People have the right to pursue their chosen profession, but everybody is supposed to earn their position. Union teachers argue that tenure helps to assure that a teacher will get experience, as that is what makes a better teacher. Not! Experience should be *earned*, not guaranteed.

Wanna small glimpse into what segregation was like prior to the midsixties? Work on a movie or TV set as a non-union extra. You'll see how non-union extras are treated like scum compared to how lavishly union extras are treated for doing the same job. There have been instances in which non-union workers were segregated into different food lines, and the quality of food was inferior. Then they were segregated into different eating areas.

What's up, liberal Democrats? What happened to equal treatment? What happened to equal work and equal pay? What happened to celebrating diversity? Yeah, right. These unions just look down on you if you're not one of them. These liberals are just a bunch of hypocrites, and their talk of diversity and equality is just a bunch of sanctimonious hot air. The unions want the non-union workers to feel like crap so they'll try to get into the union so the union can collect those union dues. They put a system of vouchers in place to prevent overflow. They can also use vouchers to get support from non-union workers when the union workers go on strike. If the non-union workers strike with them instead of going to work, they *might* get a voucher. If the non-union workers decide to go to work instead of striking, then they are bullied and get called "scabs." A little taste of those coercive Democratic tactics of the KKK.

61

Using vouchers is also a good way to entice non-union actors to work for free. A lot of actors desperately want to get into the union because they think that's how they get work. But being in the union doesn't guarantee you work. The union has just ensured that you're someone else they get to collect dues from, whether you're working or not. Unions and Democrats are using vouchers and minimum wage just to string people along.

Of course, because I think this way, I'm out of touch; however, I say that it's the *liberals* who are out of touch. All these rich, elitist liberals pretend to support minimum wage workers with patronizing rhetoric like, *You're the ones who make America work.* But then these same elitists portray minimum wage occupations as meaningless. When you remind them that national unemployment held at five percent during Bush's term they say, *Yeah, but a lot of those jobs were stupid, menial, minimum wage jobs.*

Here's another example of how backwards liberals are when it comes to fiscal policy: they complain more about the *economy* than they complain about *jobs* when it comes down to it. It's not work they're interested in making more available. It's money they want more available. Where's my proof? They want to extend unemployment benefits. Unemployment has hovered around nine percent for the greater part of Obama's term, and liberals want unemployment benefits extended. Extending unemployment benefits means extending the time that unemployment stays at nine percent. Am I the only one seeing the correlation here? They want more *money* available to them. And when you have people who are just receiving money without being productive, the economy is negatively affected.

I know, I am *so* guilty of this simplistic idea of taxation. If it makes you feel more intelligent, go read some haughty, complex taxation plan—the same kind of complicated taxation plan that is screwing up our economy right now. Liberals will say it's not enough money for the government. What they really mean is that it's not enough money for *them*. Well, what is it the government needs so much money for?

The government would have plenty of money (and then some) to do its job, which is to protect us and maintain infrastructure. Provision of jobs and charity would be up to us, and we would have the money to do it because the government wouldn't be taking so much of it. If liberals can say the corporations make too much money, we conservatives can say *the government* takes too much money.

If it's good enough for God, then it's more than good enough for the government. God asks for ten percent for a reason: it's not for His sake, it's for ours.

> Liberals say the corporations are taking too much money. Conservatives say *the government* takes too much money.

People (and governments) don't carefully watch their money. People are falling into debt and merely swiping new credit cards so that they can spend money they don't have. The government is doing the same thing, and adding on more taxes to boot as if they could make more Kool-Aid simply by adding more water.

One of the reasons God calls for 10% is because, in order for you to calculate 10% of your income, you have to know how much money you made. This helps you manage your money. See? God is a very good financial advisor.

God makes managing your money simple. Ten is like the easiest number to do math by. Ten is the most comfortable number, because the cycle of ten represents completion, and we don't like feeling incomplete now, do we? That's why God gave us that complete, comfortable, and easy-to-work-with number to manage our finances.

But liberals don't want to hear about God unless they can try to twist His words to back up their selfishness. For example, Matthew 22:20–22 includes the "Render unto Caesar" statement. Liberals interpret this passage to mean that Jesus wanted the people to give their income to government. Well, that's not true.

63

WHAT IS CAESAR'S?

Let me help you liberal socialists with the "Render unto Caesar" statement. Remember, Jesus said, "Show me the coin." The person depicted on the coin was a Roman emperor. Inscribed on the coin were the words "Worshipful Son of the God, Augustus." Well, if this dude is supposed to be the son of god, then where does that leave Jesus? Right off the bat, Jesus dismissed their question because these people were in violation of one of God's top ten laws: the coin had engraved graven image of a false god.

The founding fathers knew that it is not good for the government to have its hand in the people's pocket. They constructed the Constitution so that we could make amendments to experiment with things such as an income tax, yes, but they left the income tax out of the original model for specific reasons.

64 It says "In God We Trust" on our money. Unfortunately, people either overlook that statement or abhor it and want it removed. "In God We Trust" is on our money because money is not our source of security. God is. God blessed us with the skills, talents, and abilities to earn the money in the first place. The love of money is the root of all evil, and if you see money as a source of security, or even go as far as to love money, then you're a part of what's going wrong with the nation's economy, as well as the problem with the human condition. "In God We Trust" was meant to be placed on something that everybody would use and which would be widely circulated. It's a message to constantly remind us that God is where we should place our trust.

TRUST ME WITH YOUR MONEY

Given how irresponsible people can be with their own money, do you think they're going to be responsible at all with someone else's money? Many friendships have ended because a so-called friend refused to respect what was borrowed. Families have feuded over kin disrespecting another's possessions. If it ain't yours, chances are, you're not going to respect it as much as you would if you're the one who had to work hard enough to own it.

The government is the same way. They spend our money with ease because they didn't do the work for it. Government spends money correctly when it's spending to protect our freedom. The war on terror would be less expensive if it weren't for liberalism. They undermine the war, causing it to take longer because they keep getting in the way of our military doing their job. And their job isn't stealing oil from other countries. This hatred liberals have for oil is wrecking our economy.

Think of the people as the protein of the body of America. Money is the circulating blood, and fossil fuels are the plasma that moves the blood.

65

As we can see, because of liberalism, we have high taxes, dependency on foreign oil, and the liberal spending of money (we don't have) on green technologies. All the while, other nations are laughing at us as they drill for their own oil. As money is analogous to blood, the liberal factor has rendered the body of America anemic.

On top of being anemic, the body of America is plasma deficient. Liberals have denied us this to move our money. We need our own gas to get our money moving, just like we need plasma to move our blood. But liberals have got us to where we're dependent on blood and plasma transfusions; we're dependent on foreign oil and borrowing money from other countries.

Another physiological way to look at it would be to see America as a body. Just like a body, it consists of a brain, a heart, blood, etc. The people are the heart of America. The government thinks it's the brain. The brain governs the actions within your body, but does not assume to be the organs within your body. The brain, unlike the government, knows its place. The body sends signals to the brain when it's experiencing things such as infection, and the brain dispatches the appropriate agents to bolster protection against the culprits of the infections—in this case, unlawful activities.

The brain of our country is actually the Constitution, not the government. The government is supposed to be the immune system: agents moving in accordance to our Constitution to protect it and the body of America. Now, one thing that the government does have in common with the brain is that it is the last part of the body that will starve to death. If you are starving, the brain ramps up the taxation of nutrients from the rest of the body. We can see that, as the country is going broke and the government wants to put salary caps on the body of America while taxing us *more*.

The government of America, which is supposed to be the immune system, is confused about its function. It's imposing itself on the body it's supposed to be protecting. This is what's known as an autoimmune disease. One symptom of this disease would be liberal politicians attacking America with accusations of imperialism because of corporations hiring overseas. Imperialism has nothing to do with that. The remedy I prescribe for keeping more businesses in the states is cutting taxes, cutting regulatory fees, and getting rid of the unions. But liberals don't want to do that because it's too important to them to accuse America of imperialism.

So, the Constitution is the brain, the government is supposed to be the immune system, and the people represent the heart.

66

We're independent, just as the heart is. It's protected, but it governs itself. The sinoatrial node of the heart fires to pump blood according to the body's effort. It supplies according to the demand, and is not governed by the immune system connected to the brain. In short, the government's job is to *protect* the free environment of a free market flow, not *direct* the market flow.

Because the government tries to restrict the market, the flow is interrupted and this has resulted in constipation. America's colon is impacted with the head of liberalism. I suggest a cleansing diet of Judeo-Christian conservatism. You liberals love enemas and cleansing and all that stuff, so I reckon y'all will appreciate this. You'll feel a little lighter, and you won't believe what came out of you.

So, with that analogy, let's transition to State-run healthcare.

CHAPTER 6

STATE RUN HEALTHCARE AIN'T HEALTHY

In America, you have the right to pursue happiness. Being healthy pretty much amounts to being happy. It's the people who suck it up and make moves instead of excuses who quite often escape poverty and can also afford their healthcare coverage. If it's so important for you to have healthcare coverage, it should be important enough for you to work for it. It's the same in physics—ascension takes exertion. Going up a hill, getting a plane off the ground, and getting a shuttle into orbit all take exertion. Gaining altitude in your income bracket is no exception.

It may put a strain on you, but if you can withstand the rigors of ascending to cruising altitude, you'll find the ride is pretty smooth once you get there. Of course, it's still going to take work to maintain altitude. Give yourself the best chance: keep your mind, body, and soul in shape. We have a responsibility to keep ourselves in good shape. This is the best way to keep the government and liberals from asserting that we need universal healthcare.

It will be difficult for liberals to make the case that we need universal healthcare when a bunch of people are already walkin' around lookin' and feelin' good! Republicans tend to get defensive in this area, sounding a bit like liberals in some cases. Well, I don't need the government to tell me what to do with my body!

Many liberals are health Nazis. They claim to be enlightened vegan dieters but then pollute their body with tobacco or marijuana smoke, and, in the same exhale, tell us that big tobacco companies are evil. The reason why liberals want others to live healthy is so we won't be a burden on the State when they've socialized healthcare. Conservatives want you to live healthy so liberals will have less of a reason to socialize healthcare in the first place. But whether it's a liberal or a conservative suggesting it to you, proper diet and exercise is just smart. Stay in shape. Do it for God.

As instruments of God, we serve him better if we strive for speed, elegance, and power in mind and body. When we are fit we can more easily maintain our families. We want our children to honor their fathers and mothers, but fewer parents are showing what that means. It's kinda hard for kids to reflect what they've not been shown.

70

HEALTH IN THE HOME

This is another area where people get very defensive. It really doesn't matter if you're liberal, conservative, religious, atheist, black, white, or anywhere in between. *Nobody* likes to be told anything about how to raise their kids if they didn't ask for advice! Well, unless you want the next generation to be as dependent, entitlement-minded, and victim-oriented as this one, then we may have to get up off of that defensiveness and self-righteousness and be willing to take some pointers.

Parenting is a job, is it not? And every job can be fine-tuned. Maintain your house with your family church or something. A family that prays together stays together. It's just maintenance. It doesn't mean there's something wrong with you or your family.

You take your car in for maintenance to keep it runnin', right? Do the same with yourself and your family! Or would you rather the government maintain your family? That's where we're headed more and more, and, as we've seen, government dependency gives more reason for men to slack off in their roles to father their children. Generations without fathers—this has taken its toll on our country.

Anyway, people who are out of shape can be respectable people, but often not as respected as they *could* be. Most little boys want to see their dad as a lean, mean, fighting machine: *My dad can beat up your dad* type stuff. Most little girls want to see their mom be as beautiful as she can be. It doesn't mean her mom has to be a swimsuit model, but most girls want to see their moms looking and feeling their best.

Being out of shape shows a deficit of discipline, and we don't want our kids to lack discipline. When we have to have that extra piece of pizza or pie, we portray a lack of discipline. Now, if your kid sees you run a mile or two the next day, that shows your kid you can indulge, but make sure you handle your business. That's a good lesson and example of discipline. Kids often pick up on that and respect it.

71

Parents tend to get defensive and start pointing out their merits: *I work hard, I put food on the table, clothes on the kids' backs, etc.* That's great! And how many kids and teens do you know who show a lot of appreciation for what parents do to keep their kids fed and clothed? Don't tell me your parents never had to say to you, *Money doesn't grow on trees!*

The value of health starts at home. Do this, or allow the government more control. It's smart to do anyway. Yeah, yeah, I know—good diet and exercise is hard. Well, how hard will it be when the government thinks it can manage your health because the generations are less and less healthy on their own? Either road is hard, and there's a paradox to both of them. One of them is a hard road that leads to a better place, making you stronger as you walk on it. The other road is easy, but it leads to a worse place, making you weaker as you walk it, causing what should be an easy road to become difficult.

Liberals make all this noise about a healthy lifestyle while polluting their bodies and risking exposure to STDs due to their so-called liberalism. Liberals ridicule abstinence until marriage, yet refuse to acknowledge that a great portion of premarital sex is driving STDs, unwanted pregnancies, and a lot of the psychological and emotional problems Americans are dealing with today.

It's crazy. Liberals think they can discourage criminals from getting guns, but don't think they can discourage teens from having sex. Liberals say we should be more sexually advanced, like Europe. Liberals say we just have to be better educated and more responsible about sex. I agree. Do the responsible thing and wait until you're married. Liberals don't want anybody else legislating morality about sex, but they push their bills onto us when they need treatment for what they contracted while being immoral.

72

ABSTINENCE: *The liberal's best-kept secret in the fight against STDs*

Anyway, liberals are pushing us closer and closer to socialism and think healthcare would be best administered under this model. They ignore people who risk their lives trying to leave their country to benefit from our competition-based healthcare system.

How is it liberals are able to downplay our current quality of healthcare and coverage and convince people to support socialized healthcare? We've got to work to keep people aware of how good we actually have it.

Liberals want to skate, surf, hike, bike, or whatever they can to put them at high risk of injury and feel they should get treatment for their injuries on the taxpayer's dime.

Don't get me wrong. Skatin', surfin', hikin', bikin', and all that stuff is cool—these are athletic and healthy activities. But you know that there will be those who'll get injured doing these things and expect their hospital costs to be paid by others.

If you choose to do it it's up to you to assume responsibility for the consequences. I didn't put you on that skate board... and I didn't push you off.

A word to the entitlement society: No matter what it is—drugs, extreme sports, or fornication— the people didn't make you do it, so don't make the people pay for it.

> The best way to help out your fellow man is to pay the consequences for your own decisions and not force him to make up for your laziness.

73

To a liberal, everything that goes wrong is someone else's fault. They build a cross and expect you to carry it and then nail yourself to it. Socialism and liberalism take your problems and lay them on others. This behavior is weakening America. They have fooled themselves and others into believing *it's all about helping out your fellow man*. The best way to help out your fellow man is to pay the consequences for your own decisions and not force him to make up for your laziness. He's got his own cross to bear and you're trying to stack yours on him too? You can look out for your fellow man by pulling your own weight! A person coasting by on the good grace of others isn't doing some great social deed.

A romantic relationship works best when both parties contribute equally. You don't just leave it to the love of your life to show all the love. You got to show some love too!

It's similar in a business relationship. Morale goes down when employees feel like they have to pull someone else's weight. Many of us know what that's like. We really resent it when people don't pull their weight, and we find ourselves having to pick up their slack. So *why* are we allowing liberals to socialize our country and make it exactly like that? Liberals are pushing us more and more into a state where we resent each other. Tolerance, my foot!

They are the very reason we're growing less tolerant of each other now. We can't all have the same healthcare. Liberals insist we should all get the same, high quality healthcare, yet they pass laws that make sure we can't afford it. They call for crippling taxes on businesses, then tax the employees they say they're looking out for.

Republican officials have failed to confront this. We keep having to pay more taxes because Republicans in office refuse to do their job effectively enough to stop Democrats. More often than not, they've sided with them. It is not conservative Republican principles that have failed. It's people *calling* themselves Republicans failing to stick to such principles.

PRIVATE HEALTHCARE CONFORMS TO MARKET DEMANDS

It is true that privatized healthcare has its flaws, but when there's competition involved you can always get better care, coverage, and prices if you do your research. If the government is in charge of healthcare, where are you gonna go when the government doesn't meet your standards? If the government doesn't

74

have to compete with anyone, they lose that essential drive to be better. For example, if one doctor is competing with another doctor, or if an insurance company is competing with another, they will be driven to do better at the best price to attract you. That is why we have the best medical professionals in the world. They're not perfect, they're just the best.

If you don't like what you've got in privatized healthcare, you can shop around. But if you don't like what the government has to offer you, *too bad!* That's what you get for making them the source of your healthcare. If you want better healthcare, then instead of putting all that energy into driving us toward a system that puts a burden on others and gives more control to the government, why not put that energy into learning a skill that will pay you more so you can afford better coverage? It ain't easy, but it's far from impossible in America (for now, at least).

Unlike privatized healthcare, if you don't like what the government has to offer you, *too bad!*

75

For years the Democrats have been using the same scare tactic that forty-seven million people are going to die because Republicans don't want them to have healthcare. Apparently those same forty-seven million people are still alive after all these years, because the Democrats are still saying the Republicans want them to die.

Privatized healthcare is not perfect. We're not perfect, so we can't create a perfect system; but we can make a pretty good system, and keep making it better. The core of competition is to improve.

We have to take into consideration people who choose not to have health insurance. When they poll people and tell you how many people don't have health coverage, they don't tell you that a lot of folks choose not to get it. It's not important to them; yet when something happens to them, they often leave the bill on someone else's doorstep. Kinda like those who suffered hurricane Katrina. President George Bush made the announcement that a hurricane was gathering power, and recommended evacuation.

Well, George Bush is an idiot, right? So there is no reason to take what he has to say seriously, right? It's not important to respect or listen to Bush. It's just important to have him to blame! Furthermore, many didn't feel the need to evacuate. They opted to "ride it out," then blamed George Bush for the decision *they* made!

The local government, not the federal government, had a responsibility to act out an evacuation plan, emergency response, sheltering, etc. They didn't pull their weight and the federal government had to pick up their slack. That didn't work out too good, did it?

When the floods hit, it was hard for people to get out, and if it's hard to get out, doesn't it make sense that it would be hard to get rescuers get in?

Had the Democrats who ran that area pulled their weight,and gotten those people on those buses, many would have had a much better outcome. But nah, they just blame Bush. They'll take no responsibility for the Democrats they keep electing to lead them, yet despite the magical powers of Democrats, people living within their districts have been living in discontent as long as they've lived there. They don't blame them though. They blame Bush and Republicans. They won't blame their Democratic leaders because they know they can't. Like I said, liberals are spineless. They can't shoulder responsibility—they don't have the backbone for it.

CHAPTER 7

ABORTION SUCKS, LITERALLY

Anybody who engages in sex knows that there is a chance that a pregnancy can occur. After all, sex *is* how women get pregnant. Yet people will have intercourse, then make the child pay by penalty of death should an "unexpected" pregnancy occur. *Unexpected?*

If sex is the means of procreation, I don't care what precautions you take: expect the possibility of a pregnancy. It's no accident.

If a person is pro-abortion and has sex, knowing there is a possibility of pregnancy, but continues because, *Well, if I get pregnant, I'll just have an abortion*, I ask you: is that pre-

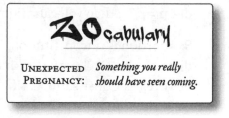

VOcabulary

UNEXPECTED *Something you really*
PREGNANCY: *should have seen coming.*

meditated murder? Well, I wouldn't call it murder because I do not believe there is malicious intent. I would, however, call it wanton disregard for life and manslaughter.

I've heard liberals justify abortion because they've concluded that the child in the womb is actually a parasite. So what do you call a child that is breastfeeding? Is the child a parasite then too? What do you call a kid that sucks money from their parent's wallet? Children, whether born or unborn, require our attention and resources.

CONSTITUTIONAL PROTECTION

The Fifth Amendment to the US Constitution states, "No person shall be deprived of life, liberty, or property, without due process of law." The Declaration of Independence says "that all men are created equal, that they are endowed by their Creator with certain unalienable Rights, that among these are Life, Liberty and the pursuit of Happiness." So again, it doesn't say all men are equal. It says all men are *created* equal.

We share the event of being created in the womb by the marriage of a sperm and an egg, which means that is where and when our right to life, liberty, and the pursuit of happiness begins. This life cannot be taken without due process of law, as stated in the Fifth Amendment to the US Constitution. If you can't put unborn children through due process, then you can't rightly deprive them of life.

If you can't put unborn children through due process, then you can't rightly deprive them of life.

So abortion is unconstitutional and does not fit within the paradigm of the Declaration of Independence. The death penalty, however, is Constitutional; if it weren't, then there wouldn't be conditions on it.

Let's read that part in the Fifth Amendment again: "No person shall be deprived of life, liberty, or property, *without due process of law.*" That means a guilty party *can* be put to death *if* you can prove in public trial, with a jury of the defendant's peers or a military tribunal, that the defendant is guilty of murder or treason. If you murder, or sell out your country, you can be put to death if you are found guilty. Liberals seek protection for those who are guilty of murder, curse the ones who seek to execute them, yet demand the *right* to kill the unborn!

78

No matter what happens to bring about a pregnancy, it's not the child's fault. Rape and incestuous molestation is terrible, but it's not the fault of the child in the womb. As detestable as the acts of rape, incest, and molestation are, they do not disqualify the child's human status.

I can *totally* understand a woman who has endured such a violation not being in the ideal condition to raise that child, but there are families willing to step up and do it. The life of an orphaned child still has a fighting chance. If people claim to be pro-choice then give the child the choice on how they'll handle the cards they've been dealt.

All the while, liberals refuse to see that if they supported abstinence then there would be fewer orphaned kids. But they won't agree to that because they need the tragedy of orphaned kids to give them leverage to promote abortion.

79

A Liberal "Take" on Life

The liberal bureaucracy has made the adoption process unduly complicated, making adoption look like the less attractive choice. They harp on the heartache and coldness of "giving your child up" for adoption, as if killing the child in the dark is so much warmer and fuzzier. To a liberal, it's better to kill a child in the womb, or suck its brains out when it's partially out of the womb, or leaving it alone to die in a hospital—a building for the purpose of *saving* lives, mind you.

It's sad we have people saying it's wrong for a healthcare professional to administer a lethal injection to terminate the life of a murderer because it's in gross conflict with their directive to preserve life, yet they have no reservations about overriding that directive when it comes to aborting a child. Wow! That's weird, man!

Give that child a chance at a loving family. Are there bad adopting and foster parents? Sure. There are more good adopting and foster parents who want to raise a child in a loving home. Quit trying to use *what if* arguments as an excuse to kill a child!

I can already hear feminists saying, *Easy for a guy to say! You have no idea what a woman goes through!* I might not, but no organism, male or female, wants to be killed! I may not be able to empathize completely with a woman who has endured rape, but can they not empathize with their baby's desire to live? I think we *all* know what that feels like. As you can see, feminists are very selfish.

I understand why people feel that if a child is going to be born with disabilities or abnormalities, then they should be aborted. They think a handicapped quality of life isn't worth having. Says who? Retarded people tend to smile more than we do! True, I wouldn't choose to be disabled, but I'm not going to take on the authority to choose for them how they're going to deal with the cards they've been dealt.

Most children are born with a standard of health we are generally comfortable with. Should we make death by abortion possible for *any child* just because a *small percentage* of children are born with disabilities and abnormalities? It's sad that liberals think that parents of disabled children should be allowed to kill them in the womb.

FEMINISM: *The paradigm that most successfully devalues women's true strengths.*

If you kill your child just because your child is going to be born with Down's syndrome, does that mean your choice is based on discrimination? Wouldn't that be a hate crime? I'm sure to liberals it's more of a mercy killing. I might agree, but the mercy isn't for the child. It's for the liberal who doesn't want to be inconvenienced—who wants to be spared the responsibilities of caring for a child with special needs.

What's also sad is that liberals are always making their sanctimonious claim of wanting to protect the earth for future generations. They say, *Save it for our children and for our children's children.* You mean the grandchildren that haven't been born yet? That would make them *potential* human beings, wouldn't it? These liberals usually don't see a child yet to be born as a potential human being, but they do when they want everybody to feel guilty about the environment. They demand embryonic stem cell research. Didn't I tell you earlier that liberals seek their comfort at the high expense of others?

While they disqualify the child in the womb as human, they overlook the fact that they demand stem cells from aborted humans. Why? If the aborted blob of tissue isn't human then it shouldn't matter where we get the stem cells from, right? Grab some stem cells from your cat or something. Or grab stem cells from those apes that supposedly share our common ancestry. The DNA that these liberals want from aborted fetuses works because it's *human* DNA. Are you getting that, liberals? It's human DNA because that so-called "mass of tissue" that you want to exploit for stem cells *is actually a human being!*

Stem cells from aborted fetuses get results because that so-called "mass of tissue" is actually a *human* being!

81

For those who are pro-abortion and call themselves Christian, consider this: you do not trust God. If you feel that a child is not going to be born into ideal circumstances, you take it upon yourself to kill that child before giving God a chance to work in that child's life. You don't trust God. I understand that circumstances may not be ideal for a child. Moses certainly wasn't born in ideal circumstances. He was to be murdered at birth. Jesus Christ Himself was also to be murdered at birth.

I get hateful comments from liberals like, *Your mother should have aborted you.* This just proves my point that the left doesn't just see abortion as a form of birth control, they see it as a form of *extermination*. It's a sad irony that feminists don't seem to have much to say about female fetuses being targeted for abortion in China.

Feminists don't seem to have much to say about female fetuses being targeted for abortion in China.

Feminists validate their womanhood by claiming the power to cancel life at the gate—rather than *being* the gate life comes through. Since abortion defines their female power, they would rather let girls be killed by abortion than stand against it. I guess liberals like animals so much because they have so much in common. After all, some animals have a tendency to kill their own young.

And what if you could know that your child was going to be a homosexual? Would you want people to have the right to terminate their pregnancy then? Yeah, now it's a hate crime, isn't it? I'll bet the gay liberals would support the right to life then! Rush Limbaugh made that point, and it ties in so well with what I'm talking about that I had to employ it!

See, Republicans are different. If I knew my child was going to be born gay, abortion wouldn't be an option, because that baby is a person with rights. A person that is gay needs and deserves every right of personhood. But what about gay marriage and all that? We're getting to it.

82

CHAPTER 8

THIS TOPIC IS REALLY GAY

Homosexuality is an abnormal condition.

Abnormal?! That's hate speech! Yeah, asthma is an abnormal condition too. Is that hate speech? Plus, ask if any parent would prefer their child be born a homosexual.

Anyway, though there are many aspects of sex, the primary, practical function of sex is to procreate. Since all of us are here because of a sexual act, and nobody gets here without it, it is affirmed that the primary function of sex is to procreate.

I can hear liberals trying to counter this argument now: *What does procreation have to do with marriage? What if a straight couple can't have kids? Should they not be married?*

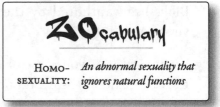

VOcabulary

HOMO-
SEXUALITY: *An abnormal sexuality that ignores natural functions*

Try to beat that logic, you homophobe! That doesn't change the fact that a man and a woman are still designed to procreate together and are the only way to bring about procreation, you *heterophobe*. They may not be able to, but they are still designed to. Homosexuals are not designed to procreate together.

The universe perpetuates its existence by the interplay of the opposites set by God. The law of opposites is what causes life.

The law of opposites is so supreme, that even God refers to Himself in these terms: "I am Alpha and Omega, the beginning and the end."

Many liberals will say, *I don't believe in your God and you can't use Him in the argument because you can't prove He exists.* Well, I don't believe in a universe *without* God. So you can't make me take Him out of the argument, because you can't prove he *doesn't* exist.

To perpetuate life on our planet we need a proper balance of night and day, hot and cold, wet and dry, positive and negative charges, centripetal and centrifugal forces that keep our planet from either being pulled into the sun or hurled out into space. And, of course, male and female.

Those engaged in male-to-male and female-to-female sex are in total contradiction to the natural laws of the universe. Of course, every law has an author, and these scientific laws that maintain the functions of our universe (that scientists cling to tighter than we right-wingers cling to our guns and Bibles) are authored by the Supreme Architect of the universe: Almighty God.

When air enters your nose or mouth it's used by the body, and the waste exits as the byproduct CO_2. When food goes into your mouth it is converted to energy for the body, and again, the waste is exited. When sound goes into your ears or when visuals go into your eyes they're converted to memory or they trigger computations to cause you to respond accordingly to what you've seen or heard.

In homosexual intercourse, however, no real exchange takes place. Anything that goes into the anus is going to come back out as a crappier version of itself. The anus isn't suppose to have things shoved in it. It's physiologically improper—meaning it's abnormal—not to mention it's a very unclean practice.

WHY IS THE BIBLE SO ANTI?

Many homosexuals and their supporters hate the Bible because in Leviticus God commands men to be put to death for "lying" with other men as they would "lie" with a woman. But the verse then ends with this statement: "Their bloodguiltiness is upon them."

A big part of the reason why sodomy was punishable by death was because it was a deadly practice. These men were not circumcised and an uncircumcised penis is highly susceptible to infection, especially when put in the anus. If a homosexual then goes and has sex with someone else, he spreads diseases—diseases that can be fatal, mind you.

85

This is why the Bible says, "Their blood will be on their own heads." God is saying that these people are to be put to death for engaging in practices that amplify the spread of the fatal diseases. Jesus Christ has changed the sanctions on that. But He did not change what sin is. He changed only how sin is going to be dealt with.

This is where the Bible bashers say, *If God were perfect, why did He make men with a foreskin they had to cut off?* That's not a flaw of God's. That's a flaw of ours. In the Garden of Eden, there was no disease and death. Circumcision was never meant to be an issue. The only covenant God really had with Adam and Eve was to not eat from the tree of knowledge of good and evil and they could remain in paradise. Because of what man has exposed himself to, however, certain measures had to be taken, and circumcision became a new aspect of the covenant. Mankind broke the first contract, not God.

That's a big reason why God called women to be set apart during their period and not allowed to have sex. Uncircumcised men and menstruating women invite a heightened chance of infection.

As we can see today, STDs are a problem, but we have developed some means to deal with them. Well, in Leviticus they didn't have things like condoms and penicillin. Any doctor or holistic health nut will tell you that the best approach to healthy living is prevention. Well, God wrote the book on prevention. And the secularists hate Him for it.

Homosexuals and their supporters claim that *homosexuality is normal, just look at animals. They often engage in homosexual acts.* There it is! Homosexuals accusing us of not treating them as equal human beings, yet they're okay with comparing them-selves to animals. Animals also commit incest and genocide, ingest urine and feces, eat rotting flesh, and eat their own young. Are these good too?

I'm not saying all this to attack homosexuals. I'm saying this because of their attack on marriage.

When they point out that half of American marriages end in divorce, I have to wonder why homosexuals want to be part of a failing institution. Homosexuals want their union to be called a marriage because they believe the word "marriage" will qualify their relationships and lifestyle as *normal*. This is why homosexuals will not settle on calling it something else. They don't want an alternative title because they don't want their relationship to be seen as alternative or abnormal. They want to be accepted as equals and you have to do that by accepting what defines them—their sexual orientation. Therefore, the affirmation they need to feel equal is for them to be allowed to be married.

86

The thing is, I do see them as equals. I just see their condition as abnormal. How do we grant the normal benefits of marriage to an abnormal relationship? Two positives and two negatives can't be married anyway. You don't marry two garden hoses that both have the threading on the outside, or that both have threading on the inside.

They constantly demand we stay out of their bedrooms, yet they are constantly shoving their way into the public. I actually don't believe that the state should be involved with marriage at all. Marriage is God-made, not man-made. The State is being used to corrupt the institution of marriage.

Activist judges are being used to trump the voters by enforcing non-existent laws, forcing us to accept gay marriage. From there it kicks the door wide open for activist to go legalizing incestuous marriage, marriage to minors, marriage to multiple partners, and marriage to things not human, etc. If the Church refuses to violate God's law and violates this new man-made law, then the Church can lose its tax-exempt status and be taxed out of business.

87

Speaking of taxes, marriage comes with benefits, like receiving Social Security, Medicare, and disability benefits for spouses. So, when homosexuals get married, they're granted those benefits. But those benefits are funded with the people's money! That *makes* it our business, and what two consenting adults do in private isn't *supposed* to be our business. Marriage shouldn't be the State's business at all. Marriage is a sacred union. The job of the government is to protect, not sanctify.

> **Marriage is a sacred union. The job of the government is to protect, not sanctify.**

So, for you liberals crying about separation of Church and State, thinking that statement was made to protect the State from the Shurch: It is becoming quite evident that the statement was made because it's the Church that needs to be protected from the State.

AN UNFAIR COMPARISON

Homosexuals want to compare their struggles to the struggles of blacks in previous generations to gain sympathy votes for their cause. Gay marriage proponents try to make the point, *Have you forgotten there was a time when interracial marriages were illegal? One would think you'd be more sympathetic.* Sympathetic to what? What great agony did homosexuals have to go through that blacks had to go through, hide their homosexuality in the closet? Wow! Wouldn't it have been convenient if black folks of segregated America were able to unzip their black skin and hide that in the closet? They might have been able to slide by those racist and bigoted Jim Crow laws (that were enacted, and maintained, by Democrats, in case you forgot).

If blacks folks were able to hide their black skin in the closet they might not have been hosed in the streets by Bull Connor (who was a Democrat and KKK member), and in the state where George Wallace (a Democrat) said, "Segregation now, and segregation forever" in his inaugural address.

George Wallace, the Democrat who personally stood in the doorway to prevent black students from going to school, and didn't move aside until confronted by US Marshals.

I gotta remind y'all of stuff like that because I think it's funny that we've got proponents of gay marriage trying to get sympathy votes for their cause by pointing to the black struggles of previous generations. Yet the proponents of gay marriage typically vote Democratic. They vote for the very party that was oppressing black people in the first place.

Liberals try to use the First Amendment to defend their position on gay marriage, stating that Congress shall make no law respecting an establishment of religion, or prohibiting the free exercise thereof. Well, I'm not Congress. I'm of the people, and as one of the people, I say that I don't believe a church should be forced to invoke God to sanctify what God considers an abomination.

Also, it's apparent the proponents of gay marriage are trying to impede the free exercise of religion, because they're trying to force the church to deviate from their free religious exercise.

Does Gay Marriage Hurt Anybody?

Many Americans are laden with emotional problems. A lot of that is due to the fact that we are a hyper-sexualized culture. Kids can't wait to have sex. They say, *What's the big deal? It's only sex.* Well, if it's no big deal, how come they're in such a hurry to have it? With the so-called sexual liberation, more and more people are becoming imprisoned by the dysfunction that follows fornication. But hey, casual sex is normal. I guess it's just a coincidence that America being emotionally crippled is normal too. Hey, while we're at it, let's qualify boy-boy, girl-girl casual sex as normal too. You think your son or daughter is hormonal, confused, neurotic and hard to relate to now? Ha!

89

So, let's consider this for those proponents of gay marriage who ask, *How is gay marriage going to hurt anybody?*

Well, kids are being indoctrinated with social justice, political correctness, and tolerance. Now let me say, I'm for common courtesy, and even political courtesy, but political correctness? No way.

Kids are undergoing sex "education" at younger and younger ages. Why? Because they're being indoctrinated with political correctness at younger and younger ages. The liberal establishment wants them conditioned to accept homosexuality as a normal condition. Here's the thing: If you're going to indoctrinate children to accept homosexuality as normal, you have to explain what homosexuality is. Therefore, you're going to have to introduce them to sex education. It is not right for kids to be dragged through sexually oriented subjects at such young stages. This is how selfish liberals are!

Speaking of the children, I'm not in total support of same-sex couples adopting. I would, of course, prefer a child being adopted by a same-sex couple rather than being aborted or going through childhood as an orphan. But same-sex parents are very far from ideal. How are two men going to show a good example of what a good mother is, or how are two women (I don't care if they're as mannish as Rosie O'Donnell) going to demonstrate what a good father is?

On that note, too many kids are being raised by single mothers. The cycle continues because, if it's a boy, chances are he's not going to be shown the example of what it is to be a husband and father. It wasn't important for his so-called father to stick around, so why should he stick around if he gets a girl pregnant? So, if the boy is raised by two women we invite a similar possibility.

Of course, two lesbians don't feel like men are important to begin with. Chances are, that boy isn't going to recognize his importance as a man, let alone as a husband and father. If the boy is raised by two fathers, chances are higher that he's not going to recognize what a good wife and mother looks like. We could go on through the possibilities.

I'm not blaming homosexuals for this. I'm saying that a good remedy for the cycle of the single-parent syndrome is God-fearing husbands and wives to help show the way.

So there ya go, folks. That's my two cents on gay marriage. And speaking of improper entry that leads to a crappy situation... let's talk about illegal immigration.

CHAPTER 9

AMERICA IS SO RACIST, PEOPLE WANT TO COME HERE ILLEGALLY

Another reason I'm considered a sellout is because of my stance on illegal immigration. I consider myself to be a real Native American since I was born here and all. (Don't call me that though.) I don't dig the hyphenated American thing, like African-American. Matter of fact I don't like being called a black Republican either. I dig being black, and I dig being a Republican, but just like I don't like being a hyphenated American, I don't like being a hyphenated Republican.

There were tribes here before the United States was founded, and we are in the company of their descendants. How were these tribes native to a country that didn't exist? America is a culture all it's own, however eclectic it may be. The tribal descendants pretty much keep to their own culture. They're not native to American culture, and many don't want to be.

Don't get me wrong—there are certain aspects that they've adopted, but these are aspects that they've *adopted*, not aspects they were native to. I don't blame Indians for

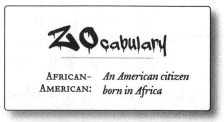

ZOcabulary

AFRICAN- *An American citizen*
AMERICAN: *born in Africa*

being sour about this new place we call America. What Europeans did to them was unspeakable.

The garden of the New World sprung from soil soaked with tribal blood. Women were raped and children were mown down before they could become strong enough to fight.

Europeans did things like this to them, but not before the tribes were already doing it to themselves, and far worse. Many are under the impression that all the Indians were nature-loving pacifists who sat around smoking peace pipes together. Actually, they did their share of smokin' *each other*.

It's wrong to see America as the only entity that has warred and enslaved.

They had cultural differences, religious differences, territorial differences, just like any nation on earth. They took land from each other. They enslaved each other. They raped, pillaged, and murdered too. Also, they knew sickness before the white man came. If they didn't, why did they have medicine men, healers, or shaman?

The irony is that we have people that are opposed to us enforcing our borders, yet I'll bet the tribes back then wished they would have had border enforcement to keep the white man out!

It's wrong to see America as the only entity that has warred and enslaved. America ends wars and abolishes slavery. But America, of course, is seen as the big bully when America pulls real bullies off the backs of the oppressed. America does have an ugly past, yet she is constantly seeking redemption. Only one kind of redemption will work.

Liberal secularists seek redemption from the world and want to apologize to the world for America, whereas Christians seek redemption from God and look to carry out God's will on how to be a blessing to the world.

God's will brings more food, shelter, medicine, education, etc. The secularist can't even touch what Christians do, so, in their hatred and envy, they bash Christians. They hate us because their self righteousness can't go anywhere near God's righteousness.

HATERS GONNA HATE

To liberals, America can only be redeemed by being burned at the stake with the logs of guilt placed at her feet. Being Christians, we understand that Christ has forgiven us, and we honor His forgiveness by sharing blessings with the world. America spreads the blessings of freedom, and she gives far more to the world than she takes. She welcomes those who want to live their dreams but can't do it in their native countries. America doesn't promise success, but she promises the freedom to pursue it. America brought a war, that's true; but in the aftermath, she left the promise of opportunity.

95

As you read this book, Africans are still killing other Africans. They kill each other more often than whites kill blacks. And when they kill, at the end of the day, are they free? They've been killing each other for a while. They should totally be free now, but they don't kill for freedom.

ZOcabulary

UNCLE TOM: *Commonly used to indicate misplaced loyalty; a sellout*

Liberals want to talk about an endless war. They need to talk to the warlords in Africa and the Middle East and stop naggin' us. Even on American soil, blacks target more blacks for violent crime than any other ethnicity. I don't even think about killing black people, yet I get called a self-loathing Uncle Tom.

Rappers have made a billion-dollar industry making music about killing each other! They fantasize about killing other blacks in their lyrics. Yet I get called the self-loathing Uncle Tom!

Let me also give you the skinny on Uncle Tom. Uncle Tom was the antithesis of a sellout. Uncle Tom was the story of a slave who refused to take up a whip and strike another slave when he was commanded to do so by the slave master. Because he refused this command, the slave master put the beat down on Uncle Tom, and beat Uncle Tom to death. Uncle Tom gave his life for another slave. He would rather die than harm another person.

The black community today commits more violent crime against itself than any other ethnicity, and they get qualified as "real" black men. But because I have no desire to contribute to the aforementioned statistic, I get called a self-loathing Uncle tom.

> The "real" black community today commits more violent crime against itself than any other ethnicity.

I'm called a sellout because I won't sell out my God or my country. I'm called a sellout because I make an honest living while "real" black people sell illegal guns to each other so they can kill each other with them, They sell extremely addictive, life-ruining drugs to other black people. Wait... *who* is selling out here?

"Real" black men celebrate the pimp-over-the-prostitute relationship: black men selling black women for sex. Now, of course, most black men don't do these things, but those who do are still seen as "real" black men. But I am called a sellout, even though I've never sold another black person drugs, I've never sold a black person a gun to engage in gang activity, and I've never sold a black woman for sex. So calling me a sellout doesn't fit any more than calling America imperialist.

Calling America imperialist is a joke. If it were true, we'd take Canada and Mexico. I don't know if you noticed or not, it's Mexico that's trying to take over the US, not the other way around. We're being invaded by illegal immigration, and they think of the children they have here as a flag they've posted in our soil.

A FAILURE TO COMMUNICATE

America is a welcoming, sharing nation. Our borders are open, as long you're willing to sign the guest book. But if you want to come to America, become an American! Don't come to America just to turn it into the place you just left! Start by speaking English! After all, the key to a good relationship is communication.   97

People come to America mainly because of the environment of freedom. Well, to keep her strong in that regard we have to be able to communicate with each other. That doesn't mean we need to know how to speak a bunch of different languages. It's practical to have a standard language we all agree to speak. If you want to learn a bunch of other languages, that's your business, but we need one we can all communicate with.

If you come here, learn it! My buddy Evan Sayet says the fact that Europeans speak so many different languages is nothing to brag about—it's indicative of how many times they've been occupied.

It's often said that America is arrogant. People walk into our country, and refuse to learn our language, and then call *us* arrogant. They leave American taxpayers with their emergency room bill, and then accuse *us* of acting entitled.

They have children here, and we educate them while giving them social assistance, and we get called selfish. We educate their children in the language of the country their parents left, and we get called close-minded. America gives more of its time, money, and blood than any nation on earth, and insults are all we get in return.

People wear shirts here that say, "We didn't cross the border, the border crossed us." Yet here they are, on our side of the border, enjoying what's obviously not available on the other side of the border. And we get called arrogant. Weird, right?

THE GREAT WALL OF TEXAS?

We definitely need to secure our borders, but I'm on the fence about building a fence for defense. Why spend all that time and money building a fence?

98

I don't think it's impossible. Look at the Great Wall of China. But instead of going through all that, why not just stop granting the benefits illegals come for? For example, stop using taxes to pay for them to go to college just be educated in how to hate our country more. If you want ants to stop coming into your house, stop leaving out sugar. If a person is here illegally, do not hire. If they are sick, sustain them, and then deport them so they can get treatment in their homeland.

Don't tell me that's mean and cold-hearted. According to you liberals, state-run healthcare is better everywhere else in the world, remember? They'll be just fine.

Now, there are many who believe illegal Mexican immigrants are entitled to cross the border because the place where they're crossing rightly belongs to Mexico anyway. That doesn't make sense! Even if the border had been drawn in the wrong place, *there's a reason they'd rather be on this side of it!*

So what's going to happen if we relinquish the territory they want? Then that territory is going to become just like the place that made them want to leave in the first place! Leave it alone! The Mexican government is the Burrito Supreme of corruption, and that's not a hateful statement—I love burritos!

Come on, y'all! Would you want someone coming up into your house, makin' use of your utilities and then leave you with the bill? Or, while they're in your house, they tell you how to run your house, make you speak their language, then curse you when you tell them to leave?

The bottom line is that we do not have a problem with immigration. *Illegal* immigration is what we have a problem with.

We're not better than everybody else—we *are* everybody else.

Immigrants are the face of America the Beautiful—people of all ethnicities here together, celebrating their right to life, liberty, and the pursuit of happiness, given by God. This is what makes America the greatest nation on earth. Again, not because we're better than everybody else, but because we *are* everybody else.

CHAPTER 10

BREAKING THE BRAIN CHAINS

You might be wondering, how did I—a black musician raised in southern California—become a Christian conservative Republican? I know, it's a formula that usually doesn't add up to a conservative Republican. But here I am.

My conservative roots began developing when I was a kid. I heard Dr. Martin Luther King say we're free at last. That means I should be free to listen to whatever kind of music I want, without being told, *That music is for white folks.* That's not freedom.

I should be free to speak with a well-endowed vocabulary and enunciate my words in a manner that is *square,* so to speak, without being told I can't because, *That's for white folks.*

The reason I enunciate words the way I do is so anybody who speaks English can understand me. Among the best ways to keep America united and strong is to have clear communication. That is why I speak clearly. Do I utilize urban inflections in my speech? Fo' sho'!

When I was growing up, if you were black and sounded smart, then you were trying to be white—as if being smart is exclusive to white folks. What that tells me is that, in order to qualify for blackness, I have to sound stupid. I gots to act igg'nant! Or at least, if I'm going to try to sound smart, I have to make sure to say ignorant things. Being black is a matter of skin color, not disposition. And when the Afrocentrics get that, the black community will be better off.

Even Louis Farrakhan is on record telling his congregation, *Even if you don't think whitey's got you, whitey's got you.* This awful idea has devastated the black community. We're slow to better ourselves because we don't want people saying we're just *trying to be white*. Instead, we have to *keep it real...* which means keep it real stupid.

Is I Black Enough Now?

Again and again, I will say that Afrocentrics who dare to call conservative blacks self-loathing sellouts and Uncle Toms are projectionists. They're the ones using bigoted epithets to belittle other blacks who try to improve themselves. You can't better yourself the way you want to. You have to do it the way *they* want you to. This is oppressive.

Afrocentrics have done their share of oppressing other black people. This whole attitude of, *You have to be this to be black,* is a cancer in the black community. I don't understand how my people once thirsted so much for freedom, yet now impose so many arbitrary limitations on themselves. I understood this even as a kid, and those ideas took shape as I got older.

It is unfortunate that much of the black community has been conditioned for this. Listen closely and tell me if this stuff doesn't sound familiar to you. Be honest and ask yourself who it is that speaks the language of the white devil. It ain't me or any of my conservative black compatriots. It's the liberals and especially those who claim to be *really* black. Those who claim to be really black speak the same language as the white devils they claim to hate so much.

Check this out: during the days of slavery, a slave's will had to be broken. The white, Democrat slave master would tell them they're nothing more than ni**ers,

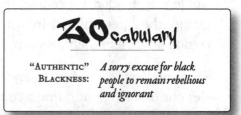

"AUTHENTIC" BLACKNESS:	*A sorry excuse for black people to remain rebellious and ignorant*

and that's all they'll ever be. Ironically enough, I've often been told by other black people that I'm just a ni**a, and that's all I'll ever be. Chances are, if you're black, you've heard those words too.

I wonder where that conditioning came from. Oh yeah, Democrats wanting to keep slavery legal. A slave master made sure the slave knew his place: *Forget about being better. Forget about learning how to read. Reading and being educated is for whites only, boy. You tryin' to be white? Pickin' cotton is for ni**ers, not readin', now get your black a** back out in them fields before I shoot you. This stuff is for white folks, not you.*

103

I've often heard other blacks tell me that such-and-such ain't for you, that's for white folks. According to Farrakhan, getting your doctorate certainly ain't for you. Ever wonder where that conditioning came from? Oh yeah, the Democrats that wanted to keep slavery legal!

Today, the so-called "authentically black" call each other ni**er more than any white person would dare to do. Ever wonder where that conditioning came from? Oh yeah, Democrats that wanted to keep slavery legal.

Blacks have been conditioned to hate each other and be seen as ugly, ignorant, and subhuman. The Democrats wanting to keep slavery legal had to keep them in that mindset so they wouldn't have any self respect or respect for each other. That way, they would stay divided. Of course, the Democrats had to try to disqualify their personhood in order to make the case that they could make them their property.

That mindset continues today as the black community carries out more violent crime against itself than any ethnicity in America—blacks disregarding the humanity of other blacks. Ever wonder where that conditioning came from? Oh yeah, Democrats wanting to keep slavery legal.

"BLACK" CHRISTIANITY

Blacks even have had the Democratic interpretation of Christianity imposed on them. Their teaching has kept the black community in a state of loathsome envy for those who do obtain riches. God has a problem with people who value the world more than Him. But the Bible speaks more of God wanting us to be blessed abundantly and be prosperous, and He loves those who use their blessings to be blessings to others. When that happens, God keeps your blessings perpetual because He sees that you are not selfish and do good with His blessings of prosperity.

Many from the black community have been conditioned to fall for this Democratic interpretation of Christianity. Ever wonder where that conditioning came from? Oh yeah, Democrats wanting to keep slavery legal.

Just as all these thing have been inflicted on the black community, it stands to reason that the black community has been conditioned to adopt the political ideology of the same ones who have conditioned them with everything else I just mentioned. Yes, black people have been conditioned to be Democrats. Yeah, that's right. They still have you on the plantation. They farm blacks for votes like ballot cattle. Democrats claim to be in the black community's corner, but the truth is, they've been *cornering* the black community.

So, to a degree, I agree with Farrakhan that whitey still has you. If we're talkin' about white Democrats. Democrats spread prejudice against Republicans, saying that they're for the rich and that the Democrats are for the poor.

> **Democrats still have you on the plantation. They farm blacks for votes like ballot cattle.**

Let's examine that. If Republicans are for the rich, that must mean they need the rich. And if the Republicans want to stay in power, then they need to keep the rich that way. Also, if the Republicans want more power, then they need more rich people. It ain't going to do them too much good only having a few wealthy people voting for them.

So, it would make sense that if the Republicans want more power, they have to make more people rich so they can get votes from more people. Because the Republicans are for the rich, they need more rich people to get more votes.

Well, let's be fair, Democrats. If you want to accuse Republicans of being for the rich, while Democrats are for the poor, then that must mean Democrats need the poor. If Democrats want to stay in power, then they need to make sure poor people stay in poverty. Also, if the Democrats want more power, then they need more poor people.

If the Republicans want more power, how do they do it? By promoting wealth! This is done by protecting an environment that is friendly to the growth of business and, of course, job creation.

That's so evil! The Republicans want more power, so they're going to have to help poor people become rich too! Whereas the good-guy Democrats are for the poor people, so they're going to tax rich people until everyone's the same—poor!

You can see that this doesn't improve anybody's situation, but the Democrats succeed by pandering. In the black community, this is a prominent prejudice: Democrats are for the poor and Republicans are for the rich.

This is stuff that children think. Children are brainwashed in elementary school by liberal teachers to believe these things. I remember hearing that prejudiced statement even when I was in elementary school. Liberals and Afrocentrics would reinforce my beliefs with their hatred.

They would tell me, *You just a boot lickin' Uncle Tom... a white-washed house ni**a who needs to get back out with the rest of us field ni**as!* (Notice they think they're still in the fields—a place they've never been.) But they'll go with those statements and tell me I need to have some sense knocked into me!

Part of the reason why many in the black community won't side with Republicans is because they don't want to be subjected to the hostility of liberals and Afrocentrics.

GOTTA BE BRAINWASHED TO BE REPUBLICAN?

I get accused of being brainwashed by white people for being a Republican. Look, I was raised in the public school system of California, which is a very liberal state. I'm a musician, which means I've spent years around liberals. If I were truly brain-washed by white people, *I would be a liberal.*

106

Most of the Republicans I know are in interracial relationships. How racist could Republicans be? I know plenty of Republican white women who are married to black men, Hispanic men, Asian men, and the same for White Republican men, being married to women of different races, and every other variation.

Dr. Martin Luther King told us of his dream—that he hoped for a day where we wouldn't be judged by the color of our skin, but by the content of our character. If the black community reveres MLK as much as they claim to, why do they disregard one of his most paramount statements?

My wife and I married each other based on our character, not our skin color. I thought judging the content of character was the vision of MLK that we celebrate, but when black people live the dream, other black people get mad.

The judgmental looks my wife and I get come from blacks more often than from whites, and that's if we get any judgmental looks from whites *at all*.

I love my conservative women of color who aren't sour about who I married, because they're well adjusted enough to know that I married for love and not for skin color. If my wife were black, and had the same qualities, I would be just as happy. If she were Asian, Hispanic, or Middle Eastern, I would be just as happy.

So, this message goes out to the haters who judge people like me for daring to love a woman regardless of her ethnicity, for diggin' more kinds of music than rap, for enunciating my words like I want people to know what I'm sayin'.

The entertainment industry promotes this image of black people. They then have the nerve to get mad and cry, *Injustice!*

when black people are perceived the way they've portrayed the black community in the first place!

But that's Hollywood for you: race baiters. They have to promote this narrative because there's money in it. They have to keep the racial tensions, stigmas, and stereotypes going because this is how they sell their product. BET was formed to get away from racist Hollywood, but then turns around to tow the same party line as Hollywood. They vote Democrat. Weird, ain't it?

WHAT ABOUT THEM?

Another thing I have to do to qualify as truly black is refuse to find any fault with the black community. That means I would have to assume we are perfect, and nobody is.

The haters say I find fault with only black people. No, I am just responding. It was the haters who first found fault with me. We conservatives who are black are still black whether you like it or not. How come other blacks get to stay black for finding fault with us?

Afrocentrics would say that it's because I hate my own people, but if I hated my own people, then how could I respect people like Col. Allen West, Herman Cain, Angela McGlowan, Dr. Alan Keyes, or Dr. Condoleezza Rice?

But those people don't count as black to the Afrocentrics because the Afrocentrics see them as whitewashed Republicans. That doesn't hold up, though, because if we were truly self-loathers, we couldn't respect each other because of our skin color.

Another funny thing is that the standard legends of black history have been Republicans.

Have you ever considered what political party the legends of black history supported? Let me mention a few black Republicans to you:

> Frederick Douglass
> Booker T. Washington
> Harriet Tubman
> Jackie Robinson
> Sojourner Truth
> George Washington Carver

These black heroes that people have admired were Republicans.

And yes, Martin Luther King, Jr. was a Republican. MLK did have socialist leanings, but we've got Republicans like that today—frankly, too many of them. I never said MLK was perfect, and certainly not a perfect Republican. But the racist legislations that MLK was fighting were enacted by the Democratic party.

109

Martin Luther King wasn't fighting Republicans. He was fighting Democrats. The Democrats have made sure those things were covered up, and what's really sad is that they've used black people to do it.

Then liberals try to dig up quotes from these people when they've had disagreements with the Republican Party, and say, *See! They couldn't have been Republicans because they said this against the Republican Party.* So what? I'm on record having disagreements with the Republican Party all the time. It doesn't mean I'm not a Republican.

When a Republican deviates and starts acting like a liberal, then I disagree, and for the past several years I've found myself disagreeing with Republicans a lot. It doesn't mean I'm not a Republican. There's a lot of people in the Tea Party that really have disagreements with how Republicans have been performing in office, wanting true Republican representation—not these RINOs.

RINO: *Republican In Name Only*

So don't let theses liberals sway you to believe these black heroes weren't Republicans just because they may have had some disagreements. They had far more profound disagreements with the Democrats.

Chances are, you've never heard about Wentworth Cheswell. You've heard about Paul Revere, but there was another person who rode north to deliver the message that Paul Revere took west. That rider was Wentworth Cheswell.

110 Chances are you've never heard of the following people, and if you have heard of them, I'm pretty sure you didn't hear they were Republicans:

> John Willis Menard
> Joseph Rainey
> Jefferson F. Long
> Robert C. De Large
> Robert B. Elliott
> Benjamin S. Turner
> Josiah T. Walls
> Richard H. Cain
> John R. Lynch
> James T. Rapier
> Alonzo J. Ransier
> Jeremiah Haralson

> John Adams Hyman
> Charles E. Nash
> Robert Smalls
> James E. O'Hara
> Henry P. Cheatham
> John Mercer Langston
> Thomas E. Miller
> George W. Murray
> George Henry White

These are black men elected as Republicans by Republicans. And they were elected in the southern states to boot, which drove the Democrats crazy.

Republicans led the charge of making sure blacks had the right to vote and hold office. There are many people who think the Civil Rights Act didn't take place until the '60s. Well, they're kinda right, but it was in the 1860s. Blacks had those rights back then. But Democrats would take office and revoke them.

111

Black History Month didn't teach me any of this stuff. I don't celebrate being black once a year. I'm always happy about being black. It doesn't mean I think my ethnicity is better, I just love being black.

Of course, there's the obvious question, *What if there were White History Month or White Entertainment Television? There would be hell to pay!*

But to be fair, y'all, here's the thing: television has always pretty much been white entertainment television. The heroes portrayed on the telly have pretty much always been white, from the Lone Ranger to Batman—from Captain Kirk to Jon Stewart.

WEAPON OF A.S.S. DESTRUCTION

White Jesus vs. Black Jesus

We've even been fed the idea that Jesus was white, despite having no European ancestry. I gotta say, there's enough blame to fall on both sides of the political spectrum for that. Those who try to say that Christianity is the white man's religion and that he uses it to promote white supremacy clearly haven't read the Bible.

Yeah, a book based on a Middle Eastern Jew who was born on the border of the African and Asian continents who ultimately sits at the right hand of God. Yeah, that screams white supremacy to me (#sarcasm).

The Bible is not the white man's religion. Any of us are welcome to know Jesus Christ. But I won't argue the fact that some white people did try to hijack it. That would be people like KKK members, who obviously can't read very well. They believe the black race is cursed because they believe we're descended from the cursed line of Ham. But the Bible doesn't say that. First of all, Ham wasn't cursed. He was punished, yes, but Noah punished Ham by cursing his son Canaan.

The black race is not the progeny of Canaan. We're the descendants of his brother, Cush. Canaan was cursed, not his brothers. So to be clear, the black race is from the Cushite line, also known as Nubian. We're not the descendants of Canaan.

American history has pretty much always been taught to us as white history. White people don't need a month set aside for it. I don't fault white people in general for this. I fault the Democratic Party, as they're the ones who hijacked the educational system long ago. First, they used political power to disenfranchise the black community, and, when Republicans re-enfranchised us, Democrats used the public education system to brainwash the black community into voting Democrat.

Since the Democrats couldn't stop the Republicans from getting blacks into schools, the Democrats made sure to dominate the field of education. That way they could be sure to erase the history of the relationship between blacks and Republicans, and program them to hate Republicans and to be loyal to the Democratic Party.

Come on, black people. Why do you think Democrats don't want you to have school choice? Aside from being afraid of losing government money, they don't want you to learn who they are. The public school system has been designed to keep you from knowing who they are, and to keep you from knowing who *you* are.

The public school system has been designed to keep you from knowing who *you* are.

I hope that a lot of black people who consider themselves liberals are taking note that if you take an interest in things like rock music, skateboarding, surfing, science, or just excelling academically, then you may be accused of trying to be white by people who are trying to shackle you to their version of the black narrative. And I'm sure you find it ridiculous for them to accuse you of this, right?

If you can see that, then you should see that it's also ridiculous to accuse blacks of trying to be white for being conservative Republican. It's just liberals trying to shackle blacks to a narrative.

What does being a conservative Republican have to do with race anyway, aside from the fact that Republicans have always fought the racist positions of Democrats?

How is being pro-life a white thing? How is being pro-traditional marriage a white thing? How is not wanting the govern-

113

ment to collect income taxes a white thing? How is supporting the right to bear arms against a government that could subjugate its citizens a white thing?

There is nothing that makes being a conservative Republican a white thing. If you really want to make this about black people trying to be white, then I'll present you with the same kind of premise: a black person who considers himself a liberal Democrat is trying to be white.

PRO-ABORTION = PRO-WHITE RACE

If you're black and pro-abortion, then you're trying to be white. Planned Parenthood was founded by the white Democrat eugenicist Margaret Sanger. At the top of her list of undesirables were Negro folk. Sanger was a prominent supporter of birth control and was actually strongly against abortion, but not when it came to black people.

The objective of Sanger was to exterminate the black race through abortion. What's so terrible was that her evil plan was to get black people to participate in their own genocide. She has obviously succeeded. Since abortion became federally legal in 1973, black people have killed more than 17 million of their children. Just like Democrats said about slaves, they're not viewed as human. That child is your property, not a person. That slave is your property, not a person.

This is how Planned Parenthood views life in the womb: not human. Sanger planned to use black ministers to promote abortion, which has also been a successful strategy. Jesse Jackson and Al Sharpton are the type of ministers Sanger had in mind when she said this:

We should hire three or four colored ministers, preferably with social-service backgrounds, and with engaging personalities. The most successful educational approach to the Negro is through a religious appeal. We don't want the word to go out that we want to exterminate the Negro population, and the minister is the man who can straighten out that idea if it ever occurs to any of their more rebellious members.

So, if you're black and you're a pro-abortion, liberal Democrat, then it looks like you're the one trying to be white. Not only that, but you're carrying out the black genocide designed by Democrats for white supremacy.

I totally understand why blacks are angry about the history of racism in this country, but not all white people were involved in this. The enemy is the Democratic Party which has been falsely accusing Republicans.   115

You mean to tell me that you've never known anybody who tried to get on your good side by making you dislike someone else? Come on, now.

And no, I'm not trying to get you to like Republicans by pointing these things out about Democrats. I'm defending my party from the Democrats who keep using these accusatory tactics.

Pro-Government is NOT Pro-Black

If you are black and consider yourself a pro-gay marriage, liberal Democrat then I could say that you are a sellout who wants to be white. You've let Democrats put sexual orientation and ethnicity in the same boat when they're two totally different things. You've allowed Democrats to add insult to injury by saying that the gay community is being subjected to the same horrible treatment that blacks received.

If you are black and you consider yourself a liberal Democrat who believes it's okay for the government to claim a percentage of a person's income then don't even act like you've got a chip on your shoulder about slavery. You mean to tell me that you're okay with working just so somebody else can claim a percentage of what you worked for?

A lot of people whine about being a slave to their jobs, which is stupid. Because their job gives them money for their service, and they're free to quit if they don't like their job. But it's the government that forcefully takes what a person has worked hard for.

You should be mad at the government, not your job. At least your job pays you. But you're okay with the government coming in and taking what you worked for. I guess that wouldn't make you trying to be white. No, I guess it would make you one of those house Negroes that you accuse us of being: *It's okay government, you can come in and take what I worked so hard for.*

If you are black and consider yourself a liberal Democrat that supports gun control, then I could say to you that, not only do you want to be white, but you invite the possibility of Democrats putting blacks back into slavery.

The Second Amendment was put in place so that the people could protect themselves from a government that would try to subjugate them. Throughout history, governments would disarm their citizens with weapons bans, leaving the people defenseless against a tyrannical government. Now, in America, people are ignoring history and encouraging the government to ban weapons. This would make us defenseless against our government. *Oh, that's ridiculous. Our government would never become a threat to us.* Yeah, that's never been said before.

Tyrannical governments in history have always said disarmament creates a more peaceful society. But when everyone else is forced to disarm, criminals will still get weapons illegally, and then law-abiding citizens are defenseless against both lawbreakers and the government. Way more peaceful—for criminals and tyrants, that is.

KILLER CLARK

I wanna share this with ya: the first Republican I ever met was a burly white guy back in the late 70s when I lived in Delman Heights of San Bernardino County, CA (also known as Da Hood).

He lived across the street from us. He studied Jiu Jitsu, and when he was a young wrestler he was nicknamed Killer Clark. But this guy killed the stereotype I would hear in the future about Republicans being sexist, bigoted homophobes.

117

He wasn't a bigot. He adored my mom and he treated us with love and respect. He tried to enrich my life with music, martial arts, etc.

He wasn't sexist. He was right there, supporting my mom with her dreams. My mom loved Middle Eastern dance, and he did what he could to get her to seminars, Middle Eastern culture fairs, you name it. He made sure she was there if she wanted to go. Neither was he homophobic. His son was gay, and I never saw him reject his son.

He would talk to me about the value of work, and that, if the government actually valued hard work like they claimed to, then they wouldn't steal the fruits of people's labor to give to others who don't work to earn their own fruits.

He said, *If you want something, work for it. Be independent and don't leech off others.* That made total sense to me because, when we were living in Delman Heights, our house was broken into on a few occasions by people who refused to work for what they wanted.

So the seed of conservatism was planted. When he was gone, I lost a good father figure, and though my mom did the best she could, his role was never filled.

The liberal government likes this kind of situation, though. It gives them more leverage on getting more taxes using the plight of the single mom. The liberal government wants to control how kids are raised—*it* wants to be the father figure. So kids grow up conditioned to keep Democrats in power.

Part of that social engineering is the entitlement mentality. That mentality makes kids happy to vote Democrat when they come of age. Their social engineering makes the role of a father seem unimportant. My eyes were opened to this cycle even as a kid. Even when I fell in line with the entitlement mentality, something in the back of my head knew it wasn't right.

If kids can't wait 'til they're grown and married to have sex, chances are good they won't wait to put on a condom either.

But I no longer had that one Republican influence, and I was left surrounded by liberalism. But those conservative roots were just dormant, not dead.

My mom was a single parent. My sisters are single parents. Sex education hasn't helped. If a kid is having sex, they know pregnancy is a possibility. If kids can't wait 'til they're grown and married to have sex, chances are good they won't wait to put on a condom either. If I'm wrong, then what's up with all the teen pregnancies? The liberal teachers say, *We can' stop them from having sex, so we might as well show them how to make it safe.*

RAWNG! You discourage it. These teachers are so self-righteous. They think they're enlightened for showing kids how to have responsible sex. Then kids just end up having kids. The schools start increasing in population, then the teachers complain about overcrowding—a problem they helped to create! It's getting to a point where kids are going to be seeing their own kids between classes. *Hi mom! Where's dad?*

What's the teacher's answer to this problem? They've been allowing girls to be taken out of school to have abortions without parental knowledge. These high school kids have practically no life experience to teach their kids, and the burden of raising these kids is passed on to the teachers, and the cycle continues.

119

These examples continue affirming that being a conservative was the right choice for me.

I wanna wrap up with this word to the Afrocentrics. It doesn't make sense to boast about being the strong black man while whining about how much power the white man has over you. It's long past time we stop playing the victim. The Republican black men I mentioned earlier went from slavery to business men to elected office in their lifetime, and they faced *far greater* adversity than we do now.

All your whining just makes the black community look like a bunch of sissies. You whine about how all the white folks have the jobs, yet you bunch up in the black community and don't want to branch out and compete for those jobs.

Stop looking for a handicap with affirmative action. Things like this call our qualifications into question. You want to boast about how strong the black race is, yet you insist that you can't make it unless the white man does you favors? You don't want to be treated different for being black, unless of course it's to get special treatment.

We all need a helping hand sometimes. It's good that we can be there for each other—white, black, and anyone in between. But too many people in the black community are ruining their lives expecting white people to do something for the black community that they can do themselves. One of the best things the black community can do for itself is stop trying to define itself as victimized. Stop trying to paint yourselves in chains. Stop hating blacks who have truly overcome racism. Stop looking for reparations from whites.

Black brothers, stop portraying yourselves as victims! Stop trying to paint yourselves in chains!

This great apology or reparation that we're looking for is a sickness in the black community. Many in the black community claim to love Jesus so much, yet they overlook that, after all the cruel things that were done to Him, He never said, *You fools owe me an apology.* He wasn't dragged down with bitterness and hate. And what did you go through that He didn't? Take a cue from that and drop your bitter burden so that you can be raised to a higher position.

It's one thing to want justice; it's another thing to hold onto bitterness so tightly that you can't accept when justice has been

120

served. To my black people, you've already gotten the best thing you can get: freedom. That's a God-given gift. At the same time, though, you are slaves to your mind, which manifests itself as your own oppressive reality.

The hand of the black conservatives are out to you. Why not take the chains off your brains and join us? It doesn't make you a sellout. You sell yourself out and sell yourself short by letting others convince you to stay shackled to a false narrative.

Remember Bob Marley saying "Emancipate yourself from mental slavery. None but ourself can free our mind"? Why are statements like this so widely celebrated, but not applied?

Conservative blacks don't live under the oppression of fear and self-loathing.

We live free.

CHAPTER 11

REPUBLICAN WOMEN

I often hear that the Declaration of Independence and the US Constitution, and the Bible, favor man over woman. The Declaration of Independence says, "All men are created equal," but what about the women? Since those founding documents were informed by the Bible (as was established earlier), it should be understood that God initiated the equality of man and woman.

The actions of Adam and Eve upset the dynamic of equality for the generations that would follow. As we know, God created Eve from Adam's rib so that she would be *at his side*—his equal partner in the blessings of God. So I submit to you, what blessings go to Adam go to Eve as well. So when the Declaration of Independence seems like it's only talking about men exclusively, in its original intent, it's talking about humanity—and men and women are equal partners in it.

How much does God value woman? Think about it: God recognized that Adam needed a *woman* to fill the void, even though Adam was in *Paradise* walking around with *God Himself!* Don't try to convince me that God doesn't hold women in high regard!

Some people claim that the Bible accuses women of bringing sin and death into the world, and use this as evidence that the Bible is anti-women. They overlook the fact that God used a woman to deliver the Deliverer of everlasting life, Jesus Christ! And before God used Moses to save the Jews by leading them out of Egypt, God used a woman to pull Moses from the water in the first place. Adam and Eve were meant to receive equal blessings, and of course would be penalized with a great equalizer—death.

Modern feminists go on yammering about women's rights. Who are they kidding? The only right they're really concerned about is the right to kill an unborn child. They resent the idea of a man telling them what to do, and they would kill a child in protest.

That's extremely selfish, juvenile, and spiteful. Oh yeah, and it's evil. Feminists tend to despise the Bible because the Bible calls for wives to be submissive to their husbands, but they don't read the verse that follows.

124　A man has to give himself to his wife, just as Christ gave Himself to the church. In other words, a man is to use all his power for the comfort and protection of his wife. This is the man Christ wants women to submit to: a man who gives himself to her. Husbands and wives living like this minister by example, which pleases God.

Feminist women ain't willing to hear that. They don't want to hear anything at all about a man being over them, and in their defiance they try to show their power over men by killing children.

They don't see their power in being the gate that life comes through. They see their strength in having the power and authority to cancel life at the gate.

So, when feminists say they want equal rights, they're not really looking for equal rights. If they truly desired equal rights, then they would support the rights of unborn children too, starting with their right to live. If they truly were for equality they wouldn't be trying to exalt themselves over man's dominion with abortion.

> Feminists aren't really looking for equal rights. If they were, they would support the rights of unborn children.

Men and women are intellectual equals, but, in general, men are stronger and faster. That makes us the physically dominant organism. This doesn't mean that we should gloat even for a moment. A real man uses his status for good, and works to keeps his spouse comfortable. He answers to God for guidance on how to be a blessing to his wife, because if he tries to do it on his own, he'll be a failure as a husband, father, and citizen. Yes, there are men out there who are real jerks—even Christian men. These men, Christian or not, aren't following God's instructions. That's not God's fault.

125

It's shameful, and I can totally understand why women have become bitter towards men. A lot of men have been oppressive, abusive, chauvinistic, objectifying, and so on. Long before black people had it rough, women of all nations were abused. Almost immediately after Eden, women have been the objects of subjugation, and today, young women are stolen for sex trafficking.

A real man acknowledges the things women have been through and understands that women have not been properly treated. A godly man wants to be an instrument of God, adding joy to his wife's life instead of telling her to shut her yap.

Now, abusive men come from all ethnicities, religions, and parties. In American history the ones who made it legal to be a jerk to women were in the Democratic Party. The ones making big money by objectifying women vote for the Democratic Party.

When you hear music with misogynistic lyrics addressing women as four-letter words and four-legged animals, you can be sure that these people vote for Democrats. It's so weird that militant feminists hate the objectification of women, yet they allow themselves to be objectified through their so-called "liberation."

ALL THE SINGLE LADIES

Liberal Democratic women promote the idea that they're strong and independent and don't need a man. And if they don't celebrate their validity as a woman by aborting a child, then they can do the other thing that supposedly validates their female power: they can be celebrated for being single moms, showing that they can raise that kid on their own. Yet, despite that "independent" spirit, they often find themselves dependent on the taxpayer to help them take care of their kids.

126

Women like Whoopie want to stomp on their soapbox talking about how they're so sick of people's opinion of single parents, and how some children turned out okay with single parents. There's some truth to that, but life on this earth is too short to live a merely *okay* life.

I was raised by a single mother. I saw what she had to go through. I see what my sisters go through being single mothers. It's hard, and I wouldn't wish it on any mother. So instead of pandering to women and celebrating their single motherhood, I would rather promote them being married and raising children with their husbands. Apparently I'm heartless if I say that, but no, what's heartless is promoting generations of kids being raised by single parents.

I am aware that there are some great dads out there who weren't able to make it work with the mothers of their children, and vice versa. Not every dad who isn't with the mother is a deadbeat dad. There are great single dads as well as great single moms.

This is what single parenthood has come to since liberalism began turbo charging the erosion of marriage fifty years ago. These statistics come from sources such as the US Department of Health & Human Services, Bureau of the Census, and Center for Disease Control. You libs oughta like that—they're government agencies.

Children from fatherless homes account for:

> 63% of youth suicides.
> 71% of pregnant teenagers.
> 90% of all homeless and runaway children.
> 70% of juveniles in state-operated institutions.
> 85% of all children that exhibit behavioral disorders.
> 80% of rapists motivated with displaced anger.
> 71% of all high school dropouts.
> 75% of all adolescent patients in chemical abuse centers.
> 85% of all youths sitting in prisons.

127

It's sad that the liberal government knows these stats, yet still goes through the motions of trying to take the place of fathers. Plus, people like Whoopi Goldberg and Joy Behar vote people with this mentality into government and encourage others to do the same.

That's heartless. What matters to them is the applause they get for having lil' hissy fits. What's heartless is that the single mom demographic is a market for them, and they make money by exploiting that market.

WOMEN CAN BE ILLOGICAL—
THEY'RE CALLED FEMINISTS

Feminists are the kind of women who believe that an underage girl is mature enough to decide to have sex, and if she gets pregnant she's mature enough to decide to have an abortion without her parent's knowledge or consent. But they believe Justin Bieber is too young to have an opinion because he's pro-life.

Liberals say Sarah Palin is a hypocrite because her daughter Bristol started parenthood as an unwed teen, even though she is a proponent of abstinence until marriage.

Sarah Palin didn't *tell* Bristol to go get drunk and have sex out of wedlock and become an unwed mother while telling other people that they should abstain from sex. Liberals who want to come down on Bristol Palin for being an unwed teen mother are the real hypocrites. The president they fawn over was born to an unwed teen mother.

It's kinda like Afrocentrics who believe that blacks and whites marrying is an abominable act, and that their children are living abominations, yet they love Obama despite his having a black father and a white mother.

Todd and Sarah Palin tried to instill the value of marriage before sex in Bristol, but Bristol chose to disregard the teachings. Only a fool would try to call this hypocrisy.

God isn't a failure for our shortcomings either. If God says don't eat from that tree, because if you do, you'll die, is it His fault when we disobey? What's God supposed to do, put a shock collar on us? God did His part to warn them, but they didn't follow His instructions. That's not God's fault.

As I've alluded to earlier, Satan is at the root of feminism. There are those feminists who subscribe to the myth of Lilith, the woman created for Adam before Eve. Lilith is a tool that Satan uses to ratchet up the pride of women and lead them away from God. Eve is the real creation, and Satan worked on her pride as well. Think about it: Satan didn't focus this conversation on Adam. He focused on Eve.

When Satan accused God of holding out on Eve, it was a reminder that God was over Eve, and Eve envied God's knowledge and power. She felt

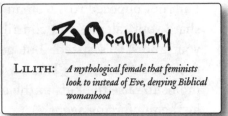

LILITH: *A mythological female that feminists look to instead of Eve, denying Biblical womanhood*

insignificant and didn't want to be. Despite the glorious standing she had with God already, it wasn't enough. She was easily lead away from God because the pride of Satan was contagious and it infected her. A fever of feminism broke out within her, and she deviated from God. There is no reason for women to be against God. God was good to Eve, just as He was good to Adam.

129

On the other hand, many post-Eden men have been pretty crappy to women. They want women to be submissive to them, but don't want to honor the other end of the deal. And might I point out that it commands wives to submit *to their own husbands*, not for all women to be submissive to all men.

In other words, the Bible is saying that a woman is obliged to be submissive only to one man—*her* man. Every other man can kiss her grits, and the one man that she submits to has to give himself to her as a husband. Also notice that it says, "Wives, be subject to your own husbands." The person being addressed here is the woman. Don't you hear that God knows only a woman can do this thing? Nobody can make a woman submit. Only a wife can submit herself. Yeah, the Bible is totally oppressive to women.

The consequence of men not loving their wives is bitter women. The reaction of many women comes in the form of promiscuity, alcoholism, abortion, or neglect.

I am not opposed to a woman having a career. Get out there, share your talents, and contribute to society. More power to you, and God's speed. But generally speaking, women are designed to nurture. That's why it's generally better for the moms to raise the kids in the early years and for the father to be the reinforcing agent.

Lucy Stone is an example of a woman who was subjected to an oppressive interpretation of the verse that says "Wives, be subject to your own husbands." It was so oppressive in her life that she couldn't even see beyond that verse. She felt like she had to learn Greek and Hebrew to learn its true meaning, yet all she had to do was read one more verse.

Think about it: that's all she had to do to learn its meaning, but God used what she didn't see for a greater purpose. Lucy Stone became an abolitionist, which of course means she leaned Republican. Being an abolitionist pretty much meant that you were a Republican when the party was founded, and there were very few supposed abolitionists like Susan B. Anthony.

Susan B. Anthony opposed black suffrage, thinking it wasn't fair that black males could vote but women couldn't. As far as she was concerned, if women couldn't vote, black men shouldn't either.

Real abolitionists didn't think that way. Abolitionists like the radical John Brown died for the cause of abolition. If he could give his life for a greater cause, then Susan B. Anthony should have been able to see the bigger picture too. Harriett Tubman worked alongside John Brown in the cause of abolition. Julie Howe saw the bigger picture too. She was an abolitionist in the league of Lucy Stone. Howe wrote the "Battle Hymn of the Republic," set to the tune of "John Brown's Body."

She and Lucy Stone both agreed that, if the amendment that gave black men the right to vote passed at the federal level, it would help get women the right to vote, because black men would use their voting power to add to the movement to get women their voting rights. Evidently it worked! There was much discourse surrounding the right of blacks to vote and women's rights.

Just as the Republican Party stood for blacks to enjoy all the rights protected by the Constitution, they supported those protections for women as well. From the right to vote to equal work and equal pay, the Republican Party has always predominantly been in favor of women's rights. In the same vein, the Republican platform does not support a women denying the God-given right of life to an unborn person.

131

Oh, and notice I said "equal *work*, equal pay," not "equal *job*, equal pay." Just because you have the same title doesn't mean you should get the same pay. If you have the same title *and* you are just as productive, then yeah, you should get equal pay. If you are more productive and you don't cost the company as much money then of course you should be paid more for your work.

Just like the greatest black American men have been Republicans, so too the earliest celebrated American black women have been Republicans. These are heroines like:

> Harriette Tubman
> Sojurner Truth
> Ida B. Wells
> Frances Ellen Watkins Harper

I wonder what these noble women would think of black people today calling Republican women "Aunt Jemima" or calling black Republican men "Uncle Tom." Speaking of Uncle Tom, the book *Uncle Tom's Cabin* was written by the abolitionist Harriet Beecher Stowe. The book was written to point out the evils of slavery and undermine the Democratic Party's efforts to keep the slave trade active.

These were women of substance. But women of substance don't matter these days. Stylish women matter now, and the most stylish thing women can do nowadays is hate Christian conservative Republican women.

Women like Sarah Palin are hated passionately because she hunts. She's hated for killing animals by women who support killing unborn children. That's weird, man!

Women like Sarah Palin are hated because she believes the eternal truth of God and what He says about our creation, yet the women who hate her swear by theories that are constantly developing. God's Word is the same that it has always been. Science, on the other hand, presents theories that always have to be updated.

Evolution isn't proven, so why do people deserve to be hated for rejecting something that's not proven? We Christians understand that evolutionists don't believe in our God, but we don't hate you for it!

We don't hate you despite the fact that you say our personal beliefs don't belong in the school system while you force *your* personal beliefs into the school system—evolution, environmentalism, sex education, etc.

Kids are growing up in foster care, but there are people who want to push the belief that it's better to abort a child than have the child grow up in foster care. Then women like Sarah Palin are hated because she believes that people should wait until they're married. Wow!

The women who hate Sarah would say, *If these babies aren't aborted, they could grow up to be a menace to society.* Well, if you're so concerned about that then why not just wait until marriage to have sex?

These are the women of the Democratic Party, the women who have hated Republican women since the Civil War. The Democratic women and Republican women differed because Democrat women believed that blacks were meant to be forced into slavery. **133**

Abolitionist Republican women wanted black men and black women freed, but white Democrats would try to insult the women who were suffragists and abolitionists by claiming that they were lying down with black men. I don't have to tell you that they used more colorful words than that.

Bear in mind that they were Democrats who made interracial marriage illegal by imposing anti-miscegenation laws. It's also a great misnomer to call these guys "conservative" Democrats.

You can say they were conservative all you want, but being a conservative means conserving the rights laid out in the Declaration of Independence and the Constitution. That's what it is to be a conservative Republican. It means to conserve our republic and our God-given rights. Period. The only thing these so-called conservative Democrats were trying to conserve was the white race.

Liberals are always switching terms. Take the black community, for example. They've changed their term from Negroes to coloreds to blacks to African-Americans. They're trying to change their own title from liberals to progressives. Yeah, they're progressive alright—about as progressive as cancer. The phrase *global cooling* became *global warming*, and *global warming* became *climate change*. Liberals are always changing terms to hoodwink people.

When it comes to education in the public or private sector, liberals suddenly stop being pro-choice!

I'm going to continue referring to Sarah Palin as an example of women that are hated by liberal women. She is hated because she supports school choice. See what I mean about liberals manipulating terms? They use phrases like pro-choice to make abortion seem like something worth celebrating, because after all, who doesn't like having choices, right? But when it comes to education in the public or private sector, liberals suddenly stop being pro-choice!

But I think that most of the hatred directed toward conservative women comes from envy. Women like Dr. Condoleezza Rice, Michele Bachmann, Angela McGlowan, Ann Coulter or Michelle Malkin are hated, envied, and seen as sell-outs.

Unlike many feminists, they didn't present themselves as sex objects just to get mad for being treated like sex objects. They demonstrate class and wit. The women who sold out hate conservative women because they're envious of the fact that conservative women have a healthy enough will to not allow themselves to be objectified.

134

It's like a woman who wants to show her girl power by keeping her maiden name and hyphenating her married name. This way she's showing that she maintains her feminine identity because she hasn't completely taken his name. Good job feminist. Now you've got the last name of two men: your father *and* your husband.

CHAPTER 12

WAR, GORE, AND THE GREEN STORE

Even though right wing Christians are charged with being bitter, violent people who cling to their guns and religion, we're not terrorizing people with violent actions or rhetoric. The most belligerent culture in America is left wing liberalism. That belligerence manifests itself quite often in environmentalism.

Liberals start foaming at the mouth if you don't believe their doomsday prophecy that the world will be flooded over by melting glaciers. They want us to submit and accept their assertions without question because, *The debate is over, you know?*

Sorry, but we don't believe you. Kinda like how you don't believe us when we say there's already been a global flood, and God has already said that the world will never be completely flooded over again. And we Christians don't make sanctions against your disbelief of the Biblical flood. We have no interest in forcing you to believe what we believe. We're interested in sharing our beliefs, not imposing them.

However, you religiously zealous environmentalists continue to impose legislation, regulations, fees, and punitive taxes based on your prophecy of global warming.

"Congress shall make no law respecting an establishment of a religion," yet liberals do it anyway.

AN INCONVENIENT MISCONCEPTION?

The typical theory of global warming is far from proven, and its proponents can't even settle on the contributing factors. What is true is that we have seasons, and that we experience climate change every year. We use to call it *El Niño* and *El Niña*. What *is* true is that the temperature of the sun fluctuates, that we have rainy seasons and droughts, and that global weather tends to reach a zero sum collectively. You might say, *Hey it's not so rainy right now.* That same rainfall that you're used to is falling down some place else. That cold weather still exists, it's just happening some other place.

138 The same varying temperatures still exist, they just shift around a bit. That's normal. There's no need to call it climate change, or any other phrase they're going to try to come up with.

These same environmentalist tell us to save trees and stop using paper. The paper industry isn't going to cut down all the trees. That would mean destroying the thing that makes them money. The paper industry, the musical instrument industry, and the construction industry aren't cutting down all the trees because they *need* trees to stay in business. Don't let these environmentalist zealots hoodwink you into believing that we're cutting down all the trees for paper as they demand to use more paper to accommodate multiple languages on utility bills.

From the low desert in California, I still see snow on mountains. Global warming is a joke. Oh I'm sorry, climate change. They call it that because everybody with half a brain can see that we've had consistently cooler weather ever since they tried to push this global warming crap.

They can't prove that it's America's fault, but they hope to. They have faith that their pressing research will conclude, once and for all, that mankind is to blame for the global warming apocalypse.

One of their objectives is to prove America is not a force for good in the world because we're the biggest of the bad polluters causing global warming.

THE ENVIRONMENTAL FAITH

There's a thin line between believing in a scientifically unverified, or unverifiable, theory and believing in religious principles. In other words, our government currently makes laws respecting a religious establishment by imposing legislation, regulations, fees, and punitive taxes based on the religion of environmentalism.

139

This religion and worldview are being drilled into public schoolchildren, preached on the radio, and infused into television, movies, newspapers, and magazines. We are being indoctrinated on all sides to make offerings to Mother Earth with our visitations to recycling bins with penance paid in carbon credits and cap-and-trade.

Our government currently makes laws respecting the religious establishment of environmentalism.

We're not allowed to make a carbon footprint on the Sacred Earth, but high priests like Al Gore are allowed to travel around in SUVs, live in huge, energy-hogging houses, and ride in private jets.

Jesus is the Word of God incarnate. Well, Al Gore thinks he's the Word of Mother Earth incarnate. And these are his commandments:

Thou shalt have no opposing science before me.

Thou shalt make for yourselves idols, symbols and bumper stickers reminding you to love the earth more than the one who created it, and reserve your adoration for the air, the sea, the land, what is beneath the land, and beneath the sea. Thou shalt worship them and hug trees. Do this for the Lord thy Gore is a jealous Gore, punishing the iniquities of parents by supporting socialist policies that impose debts upon your children unto the third and fourth generation.

140

Thou shalt not use the term climate change in vain, for it encompasses all types of weather and it is the mighty term that ends all debate.

For six days you shall benefit from the labor of others, but remember Earth Day to keep it holy.

Honor thy Mother Earth and thy Father Science.

Though shall not kill trees. Kill the unborn instead.

Thou shalt not risk the life of the pelican by drilling for oil, but sacrifice the eagle upon the altar of high places where the wind farms stand.

Thou shalt not commit unprotected adultery, as that heightens the chance of an unwelcomed pregnancy that would add to the overpopulation problem.

Thou shalt not steal. Wait for the government to steal for you, and you will receive your ration.

𝔗hou shalt not covet thine own oil.

𝔍f you do not abide by these commandments, you are doomed to that hell of global warming as prophesied in the holy 𝔖cripture of our 𝔊ore.

Environmentalists are in gross conflict with the First Amendment and are forcing us to pay tribute to their ideology and participate in their rituals.

Environmentalists and liberals buy this stuff. They read all the books and put full stock in it. Yet we Christians are foolish for believing in some book that was penned by man.

Bible bashers crack me up. They act as if they're *not* the ones packing their heads and parroting stuff that was written by fallible men. They gotta make sure they're armed with knowledge so they're not fooled by the Bible. But I guess it's okay to absorb all those other books and be fooled by the fallible men who wrote them, right?

141

On top of that, they're selective about what they do and don't believe about God. For example, they act like the Word of God means something to them when they say, *Doesn't God say that we're supposed to be good stewards of the earth?*

That's fine if you wanna go there, but might I point out that the Bible says to not have any other gods before him? Matter of fact, it's among his top ten irks. Killing is too. God really hates child sacrifice. Tribes that worshiped other idols had a bad habit of doing things like that. The same penchant for sacrificing children to idols exists today.

Many liberals believe we have a population problem and that, for the good of the earth (or Gaia, the goddess of the earth) the planet must be rescued from humanity through population control. Of course, population should be controlled by liberals, and their favorite method is birth control. And to a liberal, abortion is a form of birth control.

That means they find it acceptable to sacrifice the life of an unborn child to appease Mother Earth because they don't want her to have to deal with an overpopulation problem—as if the earth can't survive us.

GREEN MOVEMENT: *Moving "green" from our pockets to environmentalists via government subsidies*

They love the earth as if the earth gave them life. The earth doesn't give life. God does. The earth is the medium He designed to facilitate your life. You love the earth more than God. It's demonstrated by how much *Save the planet* and *Go green* language you people try to memorize, but most of y'all don't even know the Ten Commandments.

But you know what, y'all? I agree with you about taking care of the earth we've been blessed with. But you people are glorifying the earth and yourselves over God. *Yeah, I'm totally progressive. I'm just all about being part of the solution and not part of the problem, you know?*

Go green propaganda is everywhere we look. You've even got the government imposing the green movement rituals, and the cost is falling on us. The green movement is all about the green alright.

Remember, y'all, liberalism costs more than it pays. The green movement is another reason why fuel costs so much. It's takin' a good chunk of bread to fill up our gas tanks these days! America gets accused of being oil-whipped, yet America gets more oil from Canada and Mexico than anywhere else.

That's why it's a myth that the war in Iraq is for oil. Great, we've plundered Iraq for their oil. Well if the oil is ours now, you'd think we'd be able to control the cost of it. RAWNG!

Democrats tell you that, if they're in power, they're gonna be tough on the oil industry and make 'em bring those prices down for the people. They say, *We'll make sure those evil Republicans don't play favorites with their rich oil friends and gouge the price of oil and get wealthier off the consumer.*

Okay, I offer you this: Republicans do not have the power to raise the price of oil on you, and the Democrats do not have the power to lower the price of oil for you. Know why they can't control the costs? Because the oil is not ours. We can't control what's not ours.

We're not the ones producing it. And if this *was* a war for oil, then nobody has more blood on their hands than liberals do because, if they were so concerned about us going to war with other countries for their oil, then they should have just supported us drilling for our own oil here. And they keep saying, *Even if we started drilling now, it would be ten years before it would be available.*

143

Y'all said that ten years ago! Had you let us drill then, we'd have that oil now and our economy wouldn't be tanking. I guess we'll make the same mistake and refuse to drill so the economy will be even worse in ten more years.

WISH WE HAD OUR OWN OIL... OH WAIT.

We have plenty of fossil fuels, but the green industry doesn't want you to believe we do because that would be bad business for them. If there's not enough oil there then they shouldn't have to worry about us drilling for it. What's it going to hurt them? They don't want us doing new drilling because they know there's plenty of oil.

Democrats wanna make you believe they're your best buddy because they're going to punish the rich, blood-thirsty oil tycoons by making them pay more taxes. The Democratic voter falls for the vilification of the oil industry and supports punishing them with higher taxes. Well, the oil company has to recover what the government takes from them, and they pass that cost on to all of us. Nice going.

As you continue to give the greedy government more power, not only will the oil companies be taxed, we are also being taxed at the pump. That's on top of all the other taxes and fees the government lays on businesses which in turn raise costs on their product. And you're calling the corporations greedy?

144　It's the government that's greedy. More than that, the people who vote for these socialist liberal Democrats are even more greedy because they're the ones who expect to benefit from all that the government takes.

They don't care that the economy is tanking; they don't care that our national security is compromised by our dependency on foreign oil. They don't care about anything else except for getting from the government what it takes from the job creators. Yet they have the selfish and gutless nerve to call other people *greedy?*

I'm sick of this green movement and how selfish it is. They won't let us drill for own oil while not caring that we don't have anything with which to back our dollar.

They complain about drilling in ANWR (where hardly anybody goes) and only 2,000 acres are needed for the drilling site. But a wind farm in the San Gorgonio Pass takes up 70 square miles.

That's over 44,000 acres, and a lot more people see it since Interstate 10 cuts through it. And I guess only drilling sites disturb the wild life. What? You don't think putting up a wind farm ain't gonna step on some wildlife toes?

But then again, if it weren't for double standards, liberals wouldn't have any standards at all.

Something most of us have in common is that we're a lil' irritated about the increasing gas prices, which also means increases in food prices, dry good prices, home and office utility prices, and hospital prices since they use a lot of plastic, which is an oil by-product. We're paying for the naiveté, the selfishness, and the self-righteousness of liberals.

Y'all, the green industry has a product they're trying to sell, and when you want to sell a product, oftentimes a marketing tactic is to point out the negatives of your competitor.

145

The liberal green industry has suckered multitudes into believing that oil and nuclear power is evil. Why? Because they want you to buy into the green industry, that's why. They want you to forget about how fossil fuels have done more to better our lives.

If it weren't for double standards, liberals wouldn't have any standards at all.

What's ugly about their marketing? A good example is the mutual desire for the government to be involved in it. You liberals hate crony capitalism so much, yet you people are the culprits totally endorsing it. You have companies like South California Edison, GE Energy, and Solyndra that use our taxes (or what they call "stimulus money") to buy energy from solar and wind farms. The taxpayer is being forced to buy into the green industry.

Not only is the green movement being shoved onto us with a relentless marketing campaign, they've got the government to force money from us to pay for it. I don't like that the oil industry gets government subsidies either, but at least oil works, and it produces far more energy than wind and solar technology. Despite all the horrific images the environmentalist paint of fossil fuels, oil has done plenty to make everyone's life easier, which is more than I can say about any liberal.

> The green movement is the poster child of crony capitalism. If it really were efficient, it wouldn't have to plug into the gov!

146

Don't get me wrong. There's nothing wrong with marketing. There's nothing wrong with promoting your products to make more money, but there is something very wrong with using the government to force your product onto others.

The green energy movement is the poster child of crony capitalism. If green energy were as efficient as the proponents are claiming, then they wouldn't need to plug into the government for energy. The free market would be all the money they would need.

The only thing the green movement can do to make money is promote its hate propaganda for the oil industry. But that's not puttin' money in your pocket, and more than that, with the government involved, it takes money out.

If Chevron and Exxon Mobil were really as money-hungry as liberals claim, and if solar and wind power technology were so efficient, then wouldn't these money-grubbing behemoths make aggressive investments in solar and wind technology? They wouldn't be trying to squash it like liberals claim they are. They'd be trying to take it over. They're greedy people who just want to make money, right? They're selfish CEOs who wouldn't care about the people who would lose their oil jobs, right?

There's a lot more wind and sunshine than there is oil, right? So you think they would ditch oil and call themselves Chevron Solar or Exxon Mobil Wind. But no! They're not going to because green technology is bogus and its positives really don't outweigh its negatives.

Drilling for our own oil would stimulate our economy like gettin' spanked with a defibrillator. The country is already rigged to run on oil, natural gas, coal, and shale. They're universal energy sources. They power our cars, homes, businesses, hospitals, etc.

You can try to feel good about your hybrid car all you want, but it still took a fossil fuel to power the turbines to produce the electricity to charge the car's battery. Whether it's a gas-electric car or a totally electric car, it still took mostly fossil fuels to produce the electricity. And it still takes drilling and mining to get the toxic elements to create the batteries for these cars, but I guess *that* kind of drilling and mining is okay. **147**

It's okay for *them* to make use of toxic products. These environmentalists want people to be so enthralled that their cars run on batteries that they'll forget that batteries contain battery acid. I thought environmentalists hated toxic elements like lead, acid, nickel cadmium, or nickel metal hydride batteries. Well, it's only okay for liberals to do this stuff.

Gas is going to produce the same amount of energy pretty much anywhere it's activated. The wind doesn't blow the same way everywhere, and the sun doesn't shine the same way everywhere.

And you're not going to have a long flight trying to ride in a 747 powered by solar panels. *It's overcast in Kansas, so it looks like we'll be landing now.* No, it's just better to use jet fuel.

The environmentalists have only made things more complicated and more expensive. If they would just get out of the way, we could use fossil fuels and the gas prices would drop, our economy would recover, and there would be more money for people to research and develop new energy technologies if they want, and by then the consumer could more readily afford it.

WARMONGERS

I often make the case that Republicans get blamed for the rotten stuff that Democrats have done, and that includes being warmongers. War sucks, but I wouldn't say it's as bad as slavery, genocide, or tyranny. But liberals and the so-called pacifists act as if war is *always* evil, and that war is not the answer.

Well, going around saying war is not the answer is definitely not the answer. Why don't you go parade your bumper around in the Middle East? Tell them war is not the answer, coward. You do it here because you know it's safe to do it here. Which means we're not the bad guys. You wouldn't nag a terrorist with your bumper sticker slogans.

What's more is that Republicans get labeled as the warmongering ogres when most of the wars America has been engaged in were during a Democrat's administration. World War I was during Woodrow Wilson's term. He was a Democrat. World War II was during FDR's term. Frankie D. was a Democrat. After FDR was the Democrat Harry Truman.

Now, Republicans get the stigma of being the ones who are ready to drop nukes on anybody at any time, but the President

148

who decided to drop the atomic bombs was a Democrat. That was Truman.

I'm not saying that these presidents were wrong for their military engagements. They were defensive measures that had to be taken. But I think it's funny that liberals like Tom Hanks say that these wars were based on racism, but he doesn't go the full nine yards and say that these wars were engaged during Democratic administrations. The point is that, historically, Democrats have been more pro-war than Republicans. Harry Truman was president when the Korean War began, and Republican President Eisenhower ended it.

> **Historically, Democrats have been more pro-war than Republicans.**

Republicans have the stigma of being so hungry for war that they'd activate a draft just to have a real good'n. But the draft was active during Woodrow Wilson's term in World War I, and the draft was used during FDR's term during World War II.

149

The draft was in effect during the Kennedy-Johnson administration. It was during the Republican Nixon's administration that the Vietnam war ended, as well as the draft. But Republicans get the stigma of being draft-happy warmongers who just like to toss nukes at people like it ain't no thang.

So here it is: Obama has ordered our military to "kinetic military action." That's kind of a redundant way of putting it, ain't it? Isn't something that's operating *already* in a state of kinesis? Usually an operation involves some sort of movement. What's wrong with just saying *military action*? Does adding a bunch of polysyllabic words somehow make war better? Does saying that this action is a humanitarian effort make it okay without running it by Congress at all?

Even when other dictators are committing atrocities against their own people, using military action to put an end to such activity is abominable to a liberal. But the most violent political wing in the United States has been the left wing! In fact, the most violent ray of the political spectrum throughout the world over has been the left wing.

More people have been killed by socialists, communists, anti-Christians, and anti-Semites than anybody else. And such perpetrators fall on the left wing of the political spectrum. Hitler, Mao, Stalin, Mussolini, Lenin, Pol Pot, etc. All these men ruled from the left wing of the political spectrum.

Liberals are one of the main reasons Islamo-fascists hate us in the first place. Islamofascists hate all of us, but they really hate the liberal culture. They hate the debauchery and frivolity of the liberal culture, and the liberals are too dense to even see this. The Islamo-fascists use the naiveté of liberal tolerance against us.

150

Democrats are the first ones to cast blame while being the first ones to draw blood. No group in America has inflicted more injury and death motivated by politics than the Democratic Party.

Keith Olberman has the nerve to say our discourse harks back to the 1800s when a congressman tried to bludgeon a senator to death. He forgot to mention that the person who was trying to clobber that poor guy was Preston Brooks, a pro-slavery Democrat. He was angry about the position of the abolitionist Republican Charles Sumner.

While Democrats try to blame recent events on Republicans, let's examine some more of the track record of left-wingers.

> Abraham Lincoln was killed by John Wilkes Booth, a Democrat.

> In 1866, in New Orleans, Democrats attacked a
  Republican convention and killed forty blacks
  and twenty whites and left one hundred and
  fifty injured.

> James Garfield was killed by Charles J. Guiteau,
  a Democrat.

> William McKinley was killed by Leon Czolgosz,
  a Democratic anarchist.

> John F. Kennedy was killed by Lee Harvey
  Oswald, a Communist.

There were attempts on:

> Andrew Jackson by Robert B. Randolph, a
  left-winger.

> Franklin D. Roosevelt by Giuseppe Zangara, a
  left-winger.

> Harry S. Truman by Pedro Albizu Campos, a
  left-winger.

> Malcolm X by black nationalist socialists
  Talmadge Hayer, Norman Butler, and Thomas
  Johnson. They were left-wingers.

> Gerald Ford by Lynette "Squeaky" Fromme,
  a follower of Charles Manson, a left-winger.
  The second assassination attempt came from
  Democratic activist Sara Jane Moore.

> Ronald Reagan by John Hinckley, Jr., another
  registered Democrat.

151

Don't try to push Timothy Mcveigh and Jared Lee Loughner on
Republicans. Those were God-rejecting, left-wing anarchists.

Check out these left-wing nations! People are throwing tan-
trums because things just aren't going their way. You might say,
Well, Zo, they're tired of the oppression of their governments.
Yeah, the same kind of governments you liberals want to put in

place here! And you liberals consider these oppressive govern-ments to be *so enlightened.* You know these governments are oppressive to their people, yet you want our government to be like theirs! You people are really confused.

Lefties are like a ticking time bomb, man. They're quick to get angry, most likely to get violent, and continue to fool them-selves that they're all about peace.

The left wing of this country has to be checked. They've put us on the defensive, and it's time to let them know that they can no lon-ger blame us without being challenged. The liberals tried to lump Loughner in with the Tea Party when he fits the profile of the lefties I mentioned earlier. And Rush Limbaugh is being blamed for his behavior? Loughner is anti-God. God is very important to Rush Limbaugh. Rush had no impact on Loughner.

152   Fox News is blamed for Loughner's behavior. Loughner is anti-flag. Fox News is pro-American flag. He didn't pick up any influ-ence from Fox News. So, bottom line, politically motivated vio-lence is pretty much always enacted by the left wing.

Then came the war in Libya. Why aren't the liberals accusing Obama of going to war with them for oil? He ignored Congress like he couldn't wait to get into Libya. What could have moti-vated him so much? Was it the humanitarian effort? Nah, it couldn't have been that. If that were the case, the liberals should have been praising George W. Bush for taking out Saddam Hus-sein's regime. Saddam had a really nasty habit of killing people.

But the liberals focused on the civilians our military supposedly targeted instead of considering the extremists who forced civil-ians into the crossfire. They accused Bush of rushing into war for oil. Rush to war? Bush didn't rush to war. George Bush reviewed international intelligence as well as cases made from high profile elected officials, many of whom were liberal Democrats saying that Saddam Hussein had WMDs and needed to be disarmed.

Bush got congressional war power and didn't need an explicit congressional declaration of war. Most of the wars the US has been in didn't have an explicit congressional declaration of war.

If the United States is invaded, or is faced with a good possibility that an act of war is coming America's way, then the president may not be able to afford to wait for Congress to get their act together. Because the enemy may be preparing their attack. That was an issue with Iraq, but not Libya.

The one who has totally ignored congressional approval for war power is Obama. Bush came much closer to meeting the criteria for war authority than Obama has. Where's the outrage from the liberals? They're hardly angry at Obama like they were at Bush.

153

Liberals will try to say, *Human rights are being violated in Korea, why don't we go to war with them?* Oh, I don't know, probably because of a few little things called *China and Russia.*

Liberals are the ones who appear to have this all-or-nothing attitude. It's not fair that we go to war with some people—we should go to war with everybody, that way everybody's feelings are hurt equally. After all, liberals are socialists, and socialism is the equal distribution of misery.

ZOcabulary

SOCIALISM: *The equal distribution of misery.*

So, Obama has taken military action against Libya without any congressional approval. So is *he* a warmongering war criminal now? Come on, liberals! You complain about America policing the world, but it's okay for Obama to be president of the world?

It's amazing what Democrats get away with, while Republicans are condemned for things the Democrats did (or failed to do). For example, Bill Clinton did nothing about the multiple attacks al-Qaeda made against America before 9/11.

Even when Democrats do the right thing, they blame Republicans. It's a sickness. For example, Saddam had a weapons program that many left wing officials are on record saying he had. Bill Clinton, Al Gore, John Kerry, Madaline Albright, even socialist nations that you liberals hold in such high esteem (France) said that Saddam had a weapons program and was a threat. Al-Qaeda was to be Saddam's contract killer to get a nuke into the US. Get it? If Bush lied, he got his lie from the Democrats and the socialist nations.

154

Bush did the right thing by sending our military to take out Saddam's regime, but liberals curse him for it. Why? Should Bush have pretended like Iraq wasn't really a threat (like Clinton did with al-Qaeda) and taken no action? Had Clinton stopped al-Qaeda during his term, 9/11 could have been avoided. To avoid another event like that, Bush had Saddam's regime taken out. He didn't make the same mistake Clinton made. And if you liberals would stop interfering, this war could be over sooner. Troops could come home sooner and many more could come home alive.

It's a fact that the green industry exploited 9/11. The left has always called this a war for oil, and the green industry has always tried to make oil look evil, making their technology look good. They have to do that because right now their technology is crap, and the only way they can make their technology look good is to make their competition look evil. Well, they are liberals after all.

CHAPTER 13

IF IT AIN'T LIBERALS,
IT'S LIBERTARIANS

I f you are a Libertarian and you've made it this far without tossing this book out or at least being infuriated, then I'm not totally sure that you're a Libertarian! I've had many a run-in with Libertarians. Libertarians hate political correctness, even though they can be pretty selective about it. Take Ron Paul, for instance, who believes, in my opinion, as Jeremiah Wright does—that we got what we deserved on 9/11 because we're not more polite to the Middle Easterners.

Aside from that, what I've seen about Libertarians is that they themselves don't exercise political correctness when they address people they disagree with. Matter of fact, they tend to be pretty nasty.

But you'd better be politically correct with them, or else they're gonna cry. We're not allowed to be critical of Libertarians because they know everything, except how to handle the fact that they don't know everything.

They don't consider anything they say as rude, and it hardly does any good to tell them how rude they are. They're highly offended when you don't agree with them, first off, and then they insult you for not agreeing with them.

The majority of Libertarians bug me about as much as liberals do, if not more so. A Libertarian is typically just a liberal that doesn't have a love/hate relationship with capitalism and the free market. Yeah, I said it.

Libertarians know everything, except how to handle the fact that they don't know everything.

Liberals tend to believe we should all be one big commune where we freely share what is produced. Libertarians believe profit is good, and they're right. Profit is good. It's good to make an honorable profit.

That's an area where liberals and Libertarians differ. But Libertarians and liberals want pretty much the same thing, it's just that liberals want the taxpayer to pay for it. Whereas Libertarians don't, but don't realize that the taxpayer will *inevitably* end up paying for it. That's gonna register in a bit.

Libertarians hear me and say stuff like I shouldn't use such divisive language because we need to stick together. I ain't trying to hear that. Libertarians think that *getting along* means *going along* with them. To them, compromise means that *conservatives* have to compromise their principles.

A Libertarian's so-called fiscal conservatism doesn't amount to a bag of snot in light of their social liberalism. I would not want a president who represents many of the nuts that make up the Libertarian Party—people who can't tell the difference between *defense* spending and *military* spending.

They say they want to cut military spending, not defense spending. Yeah, but here's the thing: our military force *is* our defense force. You can't cut military spending without cutting defense

156

spending. A military should be ready at all times, not like, *Oh, hey! We've been attacked. Let's start getting our military ready.*

Libertarians accuse us of being imperialistic because we have bases set up in different parts of the world, and that's why the rest of the world hates us. Would you prefer China or Russia have those advantage positions?

Of course our enemies are going to be upset about us having bases there. That's because the American presence deters them from doing bad things. Having bases set up in different places of the world makes for expeditious deployment should factions decide to be hostile towards another country that we're friends with.

Yes, we know you don't like us being world police. We can either have people angry at the US for intervening or for *not* intervening. People are going to be mad either because we let people get slaughtered or because we slaughtered the ones who were doing the slaughtering. I'd rather have people angry at us for killing murderers where we can, instead of being a country that does nothing. And hey, if that kind of thinking makes me a neocon, then fine. I'll take it. Any criminal is going to be upset about somebody spoiling their plans.

Libertarians don't have the final word on the term neocon. The term neoconservative described a person who was politically wishy-washy

ZOcabulary

NEOCON: *A political leaning that is socially liberal but fiscally conservative.*

before the Libertarians twisted its meaning. Neocon ties in with RINOS, moderates, blue dogs, but mainly people who are socially liberal but fiscally conservative. The term *neoconservative* was a term used as early as the 1960s. The Libertarians since then have twisted its meaning.

Libertarians are isolationist. Liberals are globalist. They're total opposites in that sense. I've listened to Libertarians who want an isolated country and even fantasize about having an isolated island where they can legalize drugs, legalize prostitution, legalize gay marriage (and any other kind of marriage), and legalize abortion.

They accuse America of imperialism and would amend the Constitution under the guise of clarification to write God out of it to define us as a secular nation. Wow, do you think conservatives are going to be falling over themselves to live in a place like that? No! It's going to be liberals who are going to want to live there with you Libertarians. And you guys deserve each other. Libertarians hate being associated with liberals and totally deny it like Obama denies being a socialist.

Also, I get so sick of so-called Republicans who say that Republicans need to ditch their values, curb their faith, and open up to gay marriage, abortion, legalized drugs, and what-not. How 'bout this? Stop bastardizing what it is to be a Republican. You're not helping the Republican image, you're contaminating it.

Why don't you go be a liberal Democrat? You have more in common with them, and you seem to want their approval so bad. At least Libertarians don't seem to want the liberals approval. But these new wave RINOs certainly do. And some of them stick to the idea that they're conservatives.

LIBERTARIANS WANT BIGGER GOVERNMENT

Now, Libertarians think *they're* the conservatives. I can almost understand why they do, because conservatives want to keep government at a conservative size as opposed to liberals who want to grow the government to a liberal size. But Libertarians can't see that their desire for small government will have the reverse effect due to their social liberalism. Social conservatism and fiscal conservatism work together to keep government small. Change one and they cancel each other out.

Legalizing drugs will lead to bigger government. I use to do drugs, and have known my fair share of users. One thing I know about drug addicts is that usually all their problems are the fault of someone else and everybody owes them something. That entitlement mindset is not going to go over well in the so-called Libertarian society.

People want to get doped up and then want us to pay for their healthcare. Good luck trying to get a *drug-dependent* culture to maintain an *independent* healthcare system. That's funny!

Libertarians point to Portugal as this gleaming example of a grand experiment in decriminalizing drugs. And their brilliant point is that drug addicts there are getting treatment and getting off of drugs. It sounds so stupid to promote drug legalization and drug rehabilitation in the same breath. *Drugs are so great, they should be legal! Then people will stop using them!*

If it's a good thing that people stop using drugs, why not just put your energy into speaking out against them, instead of going in this big, stupid circle to make drugs legal just to get people to quit?

It's also a stupid argument because liberals and Libertarians are always saying how great legalizing drugs would be for the economy. How are drugs going to help boost the economy if you say that people will be quitting them? Not only that, the taxpayer has to flip the bill for their treatment. So not only will the economy not be stimulated by your bogus and counterproductive argument that legalizing drugs will cause people to quit, it will cost the taxpayer even if people do quit.

159

Oh, and the economy is gonna do real good, because we know how much stoners love to work. Haven't a lot of them been out there occupying Wall Street instead of occupying a job?

Libertarians talk about how great it is that Portugal decriminalized drugs but they forget that it totally goes against their so-called hardcore stance on limited government because the state of Portugal pays for drug treatments. The drug user doesn't assume responsibility for the cost, the taxpayer does. So, Libertarians: we're back to square one with government involvement.

Hey, if we make all drugs legal, the black market will focus more on the minors because they're not going to be able to buy the drugs. And don't give me this nonsense about, *There's not a big problem about kids selling alcohol on the street.* Walking around trying to slang tall cans ain't as effective, nor trying to put beer in little nickel bag sips.

160

Let's also point out that kids are having a field day getting into their parents' stash of legal prescription drugs. Hey, let's legalize recreational drugs too so they can be more accessible to kids. Then they can have a super-charged pharm party.

Libertarians keep saying that legalizing drugs makes 'em safe. Oh? Hey, Michael Jackson. Come back to life. The drugs you were taking were safe. You too, Heath Ledger and Marylin Monroe and all of you who have died from, or are addicted to, pharmaceuticals.

From inner-city kids who just want to escape their environment to rich kids who want to prove they're not sheltered, kids are going to experiment with drugs. We may not be able to stop them all, but it doesn't mean we make it a free-for-all. Make it hard for them.

Furthermore, before you try to say alcohol destroys lives (which I totally agree with), I don't agree that we should legalize more stuff for people to screw up their lives with.

One thing that really disgusts me about liberals and Libertarians is that they exploit cancer patients to make their case. Which is why I don't support medical marijuana. It's not because I don't have compassion for the cancer stricken. I pray we find a cure, and I would support them using cannabis for relief and as an appetite stimulant, but recreational drug users are using and exploiting the cancer stricken for the selfish desire of making drugs legal. They don't care about the cancer stricken, and it's absolutely detestable how they exploit cancer patients for their own ends.

I don't support this so-called selective support of states' rights to make drugs legal, because that is also going to lead to bigger government in order to monitor people trying to traffic drugs across state borders. People are going to buy drugs in a legalized state to do and sell them in a state that hasn't legalized them. Then we've got state governments in conflict with each other. States can compete in the free market, but they can't do things that could cause them to come into conflict.

161

That wouldn't work with the concept of the United States. If you put state law enforcement in a position where they have to defend their borders from people trying to traffic drugs from another state, that's going to become a big problem. Right now what keeps us from having this big problem is that the federal government has made recreational drugs illegal. I guess the only thing you libertarians can do is go against your so called principles and call on the federal government to force all the states to make all drug usage and sales *legal*.

Nice going Libertarians: bigger government.

Maybe one of these days, when you're all growed up, you'll realize that freedom isn't in drug use. Yeah, being dependent on a substance sounds like freedom to me.

And speakin' of getting the federal government out of the way, Libertarians are always talking about how much they support the US Constitution: *The US Constitution this* and *The US Constitution that.* You do realize that the US Constitution stands for the United States' Constitution, right? Yet you Libertarians talk about the US Constitution as if it's the constitution of *separate* states.

You Libertarians talk about the US Constitution as if it's the constitution of *separate* states!

You act as if you want the states to operate independently from the nation. That's proven by your isolationist position. You want America to be isolationist, and it stands to reason that you would want your state to be isolated too. You are of the same mindset of those who wanted to secede from the Union to protect slavery. They wanted the federal government to get out of the way and leave them alone so they could do nasty things to people.

162

Libertarians attack me and say that the government shouldn't have to hold people's hand and use laws to keep people from doing drugs. They say you can't legislate morality and whatever. The issue isn't about the government being your nanny and trying to hold your hand—the government has a responsibility to protect people from the selfish decisions other people make.

That's the government's job—to protect your right to life, liberty, property, and the pursuit of happiness. If you decide that you want to impair your mental state, you put others at risk. Then the government has a responsibility to protect *others* from *you*.

We already know that alcohol consumption has caused many injuries and death, which is why legalizing more recreational drugs shouldn't happen.

Libertarians can yammer all they want, saying that people should have the right to do drugs in the privacy of their homes. Okay, fine. And what if somebody doesn't feel like doing drugs at home? How are you going to make sure they do it in *only* their homes? The honor system? You guys are crackin' me up, man.

Libertarians are obsessed with ending the Federal Reserve. Oh, I'm sorry—the new tone is *auditing* the Federal Reserve. Like the environmentalists who changed "global warming" to "climate change," Libertarians are changing the phrase "end the fed" to "audit the fed." They refuse to admit that they're wrong and that they haven't thought the whole "end the fed" thing through.

Just like everything else they propose, it leads to bigger government. Yeah, let's end the fed, and give the printing press to whom? The government. Yeah, that's a brilliant idea! Oh, that's right, that's right—Libertarians don't believe we should have printed money at all. We're only supposed to have gold. I don't know about you, but I ain't trying to walk around with gold jinglin' in my pocket all the time. While I'm at it, I'll clothe myself in hamburger patties and skip merrily through lion country.

The government has put us in debt to the world, not the Federal Reserve. The Federal Reserve is more like the irresponsible bartender who *should* cut off the angry drunk, but *doesn't*.

To Whom it May Concern

Let me address liberals and Libertarians who call themselves Christians. You delude yourself. You put all this energy into telling people about the Federal Reserve and global warming and the corporations, but you don't come anywhere near that effort telling people about Jesus Christ. If you believed in the power of Jesus, you would know that by putting your energy into telling people about Jesus, they would take on His teachings and love their neighbor as they would themselves. They would keep their environment clean for their neighbor to enjoy. They would spend their money more wisely, and not be in debt to others. They would tithe so that churches would be more capable of being charitable.

But you liberals and Libertarians don't trust Jesus. You put more stock in yourselves. You believe the causes that you've chosen are what's important, and that by your power and so-called intellect you will change the hearts and minds of others to join your selfish crusades.

164 Libertarians and liberals who call themselves Christians delude themselves because they try to serve two masters: Christ and their flesh.

Liberals and Libertarians consider themselves pro-choice. They say it is anybody's choice to practice marriage outside of one man and one woman, take drugs if they choose, abort their children if they choose, engage in prostitution if they choose. Basically, they think people should be able to do the things that God does not approve of if they so choose. This means these so-called Christians tell people to choose their flesh over Christ.

Liberals and Libertarians who call themselves Christians will say that God gave us free will and choices. I agree. God's choice is simple and righteous: obey me or die.

Don't eat from that tree. If you do, you will die. Accept my son as your king or perish.

I know, I know—that makes God sound so mean-spirited. But He's not, really. When people deviate from the law of God, they experience harm at the hands of themselves and others.

Let's take the Ten Commandments for instance. Wanna know a big reason why they're the top no-no's? Because they all lead to wanton disregard, manslaughter, and murder, whether it's of someone else or one's own self. And these sins separate us from God.

> Thou shalt have no other gods before me.

People who worshiped other gods practiced cannibalism and human sacrifice—often involving infanticide. People who worship money will do anything for money—lie, cheat, steal, murder, etc.

> Thou shalt not make unto thee any graven image, or any likeness of anything that is in heaven above, or that is in the earth beneath, or that is in the water under the earth.

God is telling us to not make a god that suits our selfishness. Don't go looking to astrology charts to appease your selfishness. That's like a child who tries to go to its mother because the father didn't say *yes* to what it was begging for. Don't look for answers in what is beneath the earth or the sea. This is witchcraft. This means you are seeking answers from the dead or from fallen angels. This oftentimes leads to crazy rituals involving bloodletting and even suicide or murder.

> Thou shalt not bow down thyself to them, nor serve them; for I the LORD thy God am a jealous God, visiting the iniquity of the fathers upon the children unto the third and fourth generation of them that hate me.

God being jealous over you isn't bad. He's jealous over us the same way a father would be jealous over his son. Don't confuse jealousy for envy. Envy is coveting something you *don't* have; jealousy is fiercely protecting what you *do* have.

God doesn't want us bow down to other gods because it is a pathway to harmful outcomes.

> Thou shalt not take the name of the LORD thy God in vain, for the LORD will not hold him guiltless that taketh his name in vain.

People who call upon God to justify their hatred, take God's name in vain. God is love, not hate; freedom, not slavery; life, not death. God will send men to kill murderers, but He doesn't send people to murder.

> Keep the Sabbath day to sanctify it, as the LORD thy God hath commanded thee.

Take regular time out to learn God. Love God. When we slip away from God and want to be in the secular world seven days a week then we really open ourselves more and more to violate his commandments, and these violations lead to wrongful death.

Trust God enough to know that you can rest a moment. Those who work incessantly aren't trusting God.

> Honor thy father and thy mother, as the LORD thy God hath commanded thee; that thy days may be prolonged, and that it may go well with thee, in the land which the LORD thy God giveth thee.

Even if your parents are the worst parents in the world, be the person that a mother and father would be proud of. That's the point. The person who doesn't care about being an honorable son or daughter can take that resentment out on others, and it is often the case that people who murder have had very dysfunctional relationships with their parents.

Thou shalt not murder.

I don't think that takes much explaining.

Neither shalt thou commit adultery.

I don't think it takes much explaining on how that leads to murder, aside from being damaging in itself.

Neither shalt thou steal.

Stealing is another one of those things that lead to murder because people will go as far as to murder someone to take what they want.

Neither shalt thou bear false witness against thy neighbor.

167

Falsely accusing someone can get a person murdered. You liberals and Libertarians oughta love that one. *Bush lied, people died.* That bumper sticker itself is a lie, and that false accusation is interfering with the effort. It keeps our troops at war longer, and that contributes to them getting killed.

Thou shall not covet.

Coveting things leads to wrongful death. This is why our purportedly cruel God says, *Obey me or die*, because when we disobey His laws we set each other up to murder each other—to die.

God's so-called cruelty is to protect us from the cruelty of ourselves. God's so-called cruelty is more benevolent than our best efforts to be righteous.

So yes, God is a God that blesses us to act out our will, but He gives laws and guidelines to protect us from our foolish choices.

My point is this: don't try to say, *God gives us choice, we should let people have the choice to do whatever they want.* Rawng! God has laws. Everybody has the choice to obey or break any law, and we all choose to break them in one degree or another. God has a court date ready for us, and anyone who doesn't accept Christ as his representative in court is gonna be in trouble. But all those who accept Him as their representative now, making Him the Lord of their lives, will be blessed now and forever.

CHAPTER 14

YOU ARE NOW A WEAPON OF
A.S.S. DESTRUCTION!

I'm often asked, *When are you going to run for office?* After reading this book, you may be having some big second thoughts on that! When I think about well-known, respected, conservative personalities that people wish we could elect, it's very humbling to be considered among them.

Of course, we *need* people of this mindset in office. We need people who are going to stick to principle. Too many people are voting based on prejudice, bias, selfishness, trendiness, and anything else that deviates from clear standards. My objective is to help define the issues in the most entertaining way I can while not contaminating the principles.

People who say, *I just vote for who I think is the best candidate,* usually mean they vote Democrat because they vote based on a feeling rather than on principles, and their feelings are mostly influenced by the media.

Conservatism is like fruits and vegetables: they're more healthy for you, but maybe not as tasty to a lot of people. My objective is to keep people engaged with entertainment that hopefully causes them to be receptive to conservative principles they can genuinely appreciate. Not hypnotize, mesmerize, and indoctrinate.

This is not easy to do, because, once you've been told the truth, where do you go from there? The truth is hard to sell because it seems boring. You can't do anything else with it. This is why it's hard for conservatives to promote their conservative values.

People vote Democratic, not because of principle, but because of feelings swayed by the media.

Whereas a lie is already a creative process, and this is where liberals excel. Liberals live in a world of make-believe. That's why they excel in the entertainment industry and performing arts.

Isn't it weird that right-wing people are more of the logical left-brain types, and left-wing people are more of the artistic right-brain? Of course, left-wing people think they're logical, which is that artistic side of their brain playing make-believe again.

I keep telling y'all, it ain't all about the people that are in office, it's the culture that *puts* them there. You've got to be able to connect with them, and the culture likes to be entertained. You know the saying "The way to a man's heart is through his stomach?" Well, the way to our culture's heart is through entertainment.

Now, I don't expect Hollywood to change. Maybe it will, but I'm not waiting on it. I'd rather see and hear entertainment friendly to Christians, made by Christians, and with the same conservative message.

When people see what conservative principles are *from conservatives,* instead of from the donkey's mouth, we'll have more people ready to vote with a clearer understanding of what conservatism is. I wouldn't be as effective to that end if I were in office. I gots to be in the trenches!

The person we elect is the person who is ready, willing, and able to represent us, not get in there to run things the way they think things ought to be run. Their job is to do what the ones who voted for them called them to do, not try to make *everybody* happy with a bunch of reach across the aisle to liberalism nonsense.

A FINAL WORD

There have been a few factors that have lead me to conservatism, one of which was my martial arts instructor. When we began in 1995, I was pretty liberal. The seed that was planted by Killer Clark, my neighbor, had gone dormant. The liberal weeds had grown over it. I gave way to supporting a woman's choice to have abortions. I hated the government, yet believed in government provisions, and believed we were imperialists.

I loved martial arts, though. The objective of our training was to develop great speed, elegance, and power, in mind and body. I was trained well, but our instructor made sure that we weren't the types to let our ego make us hungry for a fight. I didn't feel the need to hurt or dominate anybody. It made sense for me to develop a body for war and a mind for peace. 171

A body for war is strong and healthy. You don't send the sick and the weak to war. As I worked to see myself with a strong, healthy body, I started to see America the same way.

A mind for peace is a healthy mind. An unhealthy mind seeks chaos and does nothing to bring order from chaos. A mind for peace knows that sometimes it is necessary to commit the body to war to protect the peace.

Peace is valuable. Remember, anything of value has to be protected because there are those who will either try to steal or destroy things of value. So, as a martial artist, it didn't make sense for me to practice self-defense while claiming to be this liberal pacifist!

My instructor, who has a deep respect for Buddhism, is Christian. One of the first things he brought to my attention was basically this: you don't have to believe in God, but your martial arts training will be better if you do. It is a tool God has given you to make you better. If you use it by His design, martial arts can improve your life. If you use it for your own gratification, it will leave you unfulfilled, no matter how strong you think you've become.

Well, I didn't want to hear that. I was more endowed with confusion than Confucius. But the seed of faith had been watered none the less, and the foundation was being strengthened.

172 Foundation is important to any good instruction, and my instructor's lessons were no exception. It was always stance work, stance work, stance work, stance work!

It clicked when I started to hear the cliché selling point of mixed martial arts: all fights go to the ground. Sure, the undisciplined fighter may get taken to the ground, but the fighter who trains his rooting and how to move quickly with it has a better chance of staying on his feet.

Republicans have not been training their stance. Many have lost their foundation, and have been taken to the ground *hard*. Republicans are down on a hard floor, and the boots are being put to them by the so-called peaceful, diplomatic left. We *are* getting back on our feet, but it shouldn't be this hard.

We have to have our foundation laid where we know how to keep our balance, and even learn how to use our stance to make our opponent lose *their* balance.

A lot of people throw a punch and end up on the ground. Why? Because they haven't trained their stance to sustain the force of their punch. They overcommit and end up off balance. From there, we start working on application. We take cryptic movements, and decipher their codes, unlocking their combative moves.

A form is a moving weapon's manual. The Republicans aren't studying their manuals. The ones I highly recommend are the Bible and the Constitution. We have a purpose, remember? Every utility comes with a manual.

The Republicans need to reestablish their foundation. Use the Bible to lay it level and strong. Use the instructions to apply the principles you've learned.

As always, application trumps theory. Martial arts gained a bad rap because people were learning how to kick and punch and yell *KI-YAI!* but weren't taught how to apply that stuff in a real situation. Our instructor didn't do that. We didn't just learn moves—he was adamant about application. But wait—application must be followed with adaptation.

173

Your opponent isn't going to throw one punch and just stand there as you show off how many times you can throw a bunch of strikes. Your opponent is going to swing a bunch of times! They're going to clinch, tackle, and kick if they can. You have to adapt! You learn principles so that you can adapt, keeping your integrity while your opponent loses his.

Republicans have not been successful with adaptation. Liberals have been handing our behinds to us in music, media, movies, TV, education, etc. Liberals falsely accuse and Republicans have to learn how to use these false accusations and projections against them. We've not been battling them on those fronts. But we can!

We can deliver news with honesty and not have to resort to cheap tactics. We can deliver it with humor and style without being cynical and elitist. We can create music that is dance-able, slammin', motivating, romantic, etc., without promoting violence, misogyny, fornication, and American hatred. We can create movies that clearly define who fights for freedom and who doesn't—movies that don't depend on nudity for more ticket sales. We need conservative teachers to break the spell that liberal teachers are laying on students.

Finally, after we've laid the foundation, work application, employ adaptation, the next thing is to pass on what was learned. Pass it on without changing the foundation. Whether you draw or play music, there are certain unchanging principles.

Once the student is grounded on these principles, they are equipped with the tools to express themselves how they see fit. Make sure you teach the core principles. Do not teach your variations. If you do, then you will have robbed the student of being an individual, and are merely making a clone. Teach core principles so the student has a solid standard to go by, and adapt with, and a standard to pass on.

174

Foundation. Application. Adaptation. Edification. Add God to that cycle, and we'll be all right!

Conservatives *have to be able to pass on what they know*. They have to show the people what they've been looking for. Get the student excited about the lesson.

Continued blessings, and thanks for reading!